THE BIGGER MESSAGE

Live Your Best Life by Understanding Universal Context

Second Edition

Lynn M. Scheurell
#1 Bestselling Author

FREE – Bonus Downloads

This book includes an eBook about why things happen *and* a companion guide you can use to note your reflections and observations on your Bigger Messages.

Get Them NOW at

lynnscheurell.com/reasons-message/

MIZRAHI PRESS

Copyright ©2023 Creative Catalyst, LLC

Printed in the United States of America

No part of this publication may be reproduced, stored in a retrieval system or transmitted in any form by any means, electronic or mechanical, photocopying, recording, scanning or otherwise except as permitted under Section 107 or 108 of the 1976 United States Copyright Act, without the prior written permission of the Publisher.

ISBN-13: 978-0-9801550-9-9 (paperback)

Limit of Liability/Disclaimer of Warranty
While the author has used their best efforts in preparing this report, they make no representation or warranties with respect to the accuracy or completeness of the contents and specifically disclaim any implied warranties. The advice and strategies contained herein may not be suitable for your situation. You should consult with a professional where appropriate. The author shall not be liable for any loss of profit or any other commercial damages, including but not limited to special, incidental, consequential or other damages.

Published by Mizrahi Press
A Division of Creative Catalyst LLC
MyCreativeCatalyst.com

Table of Contents

A Note from the Author   1

Introduction   3

Defining a 'Bigger Message'   5
    Signs of Bigger Messages   6
    Disguises that Bigger Messages Wear   10
    Differences Can Surface Bigger Messages   16

Four Elements for Living A Bigger Life   19
    Perception Is Everything   21
    The Consequences of Taking Action   24
    How Relationships Work with Bigger Messages   26

The Bigger Message Formula   29
    Cues and Clues   31
    It's All Connected   35
    Principles of The Bigger Message   38

What To Do In The Middle Of A Message   45
    Getting Intentional Messages   47
    Six Signs of Not Listening   51
    Good Questions Yield Good Messages   57

The Keys To Manifesting What You Really Want   61
    Why Are Some Things Easier to Manifest Than Others?   71
    Integrity Is Glue For Good Living   74
    Commit to What You've Learned   89

Now What?   93
Bonus Gift   97
About the Author   99
Other Books by Lynn Scheurell   103

A Note from the Author

To live a successful life now requires a boldness that has nearly been bred out of us through social conditioning and emotional contraction. We learn from the world around us and, all too often, that means through the unconscious limited perceptions of our authority figures and childhood influences.

Knowing what you want and then giving yourself the permission and resources to go after it is a big part of why you are here. You are part of a greater whole that is only served by you being your true self. You being anything less takes away from everybody and everything else. It's a little bit selfish to think that you don't matter, that you don't add to the world around you—it is because of you that our world IS. Your presence inevitably affects the world—the real question you must answer for yourself is in what way you want to direct, focus, and add your life spark to the world.

There is a greater power, call it whatever name you will, that is consistently helping you—and each of us—achieve greatness. It communicates through dynamic life force energy, always creating something new with the intention of making us stronger, better, and more knowledgeable. It doesn't always come through with perfectly wrapped pretty packages; instead, our most significant opportunities can look like challenges, difficult conversations, and uncomfortable circumstances. Within every life scenario, there is always a silver thread of a larger perspective...a Bigger Message, as it were.

Given my penchant for connecting inner landscape to outer experience, this book explores different facets of life's Bigger Messages that are individually crafted for you. May this book help you gain fresh insight, personal transformation, and the power of choice in your decisions going forward.

Introduction

How do we create our world? What are we here for? Why do we matter? Why do things happen the way they do? What does it all mean?

Finding the answers to these questions, and others, is what keeps us busy for most of our lives. The single pursuit of understanding how change works, what the Bigger Message is, and how we create or deny our evolution is fascinating on every level. It is our individual and collective life purpose to discover and distill these huge questions into something that makes sense.

The truth is that we must live in alignment with personal knowingness. Knowing what you want, then giving yourself the permission and resources to go after it, is a big part of why you are here. You are part of a greater whole that is only served by you being your true self. You being anything less takes away from everybody and everything else.

It may seem a bit convoluted or counterintuitive in the initial awareness of it, but when you understand that you ARE the power to create what you want, the world suddenly feels very different. Then, once you get that, what do you do with it? And how do you begin the process of intentional change by understanding the Bigger Messages?

That is what we will be exploring here. To get the most from this book, take notes on cues and clues for your potential Bigger Messages as you go in the Companion Guide (you'll find the link on the title page of the book). You can analyze your thoughts later . . . initially, just capture them so you can find them easier when you're ready to process their meaning.

Defining a 'Bigger Message'

Your life has context. When you understand the meaning of what's happening in your life, you can see that it is not happening *to* you but *for* you. Having this larger insight gives you the ability to thrive through even the most difficult situations. It's not really what occurs but how you relate to the situation and then make your choices in handling it and integrating the outcomes of it.

For example, when a job is lost, a relationship breaks up, an illness is diagnosed, or a friend betrays, it's easier to point blame than to do the inner work of perception, which is actually the greater motivator behind the situation.

Even more, this is the fastest-paced society yet known to mankind, which makes life feel even more chaotic and difficult to manage. The result is that what happens to you may not make sense if you're swallowed up in the turbulence of it all or too close to the situation...and if you're unwilling or unable to understand the deeper meaning, your life will slow down or even get stuck until you sort it out.

Essentially, when we humans have a framework to understand *why* something happens—the Bigger Message of it—we seem to be able to move forward through our lives easier. There is an elegant grace afforded to even the most difficult circumstances when we know how to perceive the larger landscape and can see that there is a bigger picture to their occurrence. In short, it's the Bigger Message within what happens to you that matters.

Inspiration lives where there is purpose. When you understand and are inspired by purpose, you know how to connect the dots and any potential crisis of meaning about the nature of your role in it is resolved. Your full, authentic presence in any situation, relationship, or environment changes everything.

And that's the purpose of The Bigger Message—to give you the awareness of the greater context of your life's occurrences in helping you become your best self. When you know the 'why'—the context of your life experiences—your brain is able to assimilate the seeming chaos into systematic order. That means you can get on with living your best life sooner.

With insight into the Bigger Message, you understand the greater why and, with clarity, you can make more informed choices about your time, energy, and focus. Understand the context of your life by 'getting' your Bigger Messages through what you are about to read in this book.

Signs of Bigger Messages

When was the last time you felt really happy with all parts of your life? That you felt comfortable in your own skin? Reveled in the full knowingness that everything in your world is positively just the best and just for you?

If it's been a while or if you can't even imagine any of the above, you're not alone. Most people don't even take pause to think that such things are possible, so by virtue of reading this book, you are a pioneer in creating positive life change for yourself.

DEFINING A 'BIGGER MESSAGE'

The irony is that you're always receiving the transmissions that can help you live your biggest life... if you can understand them.

When people are ready, or need, to create change for something new, their life rhythm changes. There is a new cadence to how things flow, or don't flow, that pervades daily living. It usually starts out small and gets bigger over time if it needs to get your attention (depending on if you ignore, deny, neglect, or avoid it).

Or it may seem that it's happening all at once—various aspects of your life feel like they are each crumbling or imploding at virtually the same time. However, chances are that if it feels like it's all at once, you can look back and trace the beginnings of where it started—maybe the current situation is reflecting a challenge or issue that you didn't get handled the first time around for some reason.

The bonus of it feeling like it's happening all at once is that you can often create the most dramatic change in that moment. Big upheavals mean big messages that invite significant change and, if you start creating intentionally in that moment, you can often influence the forces of change that are happening anyway to bring you more of what you DO want.

Regardless of the change that is happening, or not, in your life right now, here are some of the messages that can tell you that your biggest life is on its way to you and it's time to proactively create what you want.

One of the most pervasive messages inviting clarity is that you feel a vague sense of restlessness, of unease, of wanting something but not knowing what it is. It's an irking feeling you could describe as feeling like 'a Lamborghini stuck behind a lawnmower.' It can feel evasive but gnawing, like registering a sound that bugs you but not placing it until you realize it's the refrigerator humming (you don't even notice that until it's off, right?).

To the degree you feel restless in your life is to the degree you are moving toward your boldest life. So, when you feel restless, rather than letting it spin you into some level of frenetic compensation or unhappiness, trust the Bigger Message being revealed—you are in a new movement toward something better. (Then to handle the physical symptoms in your body, go move your big muscle groups—take a walk, ride a bike, climb some stairs —as that will release the pent-up energy in your body, so it doesn't have to express itself as emotional congestion.) ;=)

You'll see that things around you are breaking, not working anymore or even ending. That might mean physical things in your home, such as appliances, light bulbs, doorbells, or furniture, projects at work (or home) where you just aren't on track due to circumstances seemingly beyond your control, or even clients taking their business elsewhere or making unusual requests. Maybe it is routines or habits that you have difficulty with or just don't follow through on anymore that seem to 'break.' A significant scenario is when your relationships no longer fit you or haven't grown with your life flow and need to be repaired or replaced.

Our relationships are our mirrors, so if you don't like what you see, it's time to pay attention to that quality in yourself for positive intervention. You might go through a time when you are communicating but your people aren't hearing or understanding you.

Maybe they're telling you to slow down or take a break when you know you need to keep going or even speed up. It might appear that they don't understand or relate to you anymore. You no longer pace your relationships the same way. It may come to decision time in choosing whether the relationship can be repaired or if it just needs to be replaced with someone who is more in alignment with who you are now. This is often one of the most difficult and/or emotional messages to assimilate into your life flow.

Another thing that could 'break' is your physical body. If you are having odd little accidents, or health twinges, or something different happening with your body, it is a message that things are out of whack somehow and need positive change to get back to normal operation. This could also include your car, which is what gets you places; if your car is out of commission, you are standing still. And it can include anything in your physical world—the squeaky door, the appliance that quits working. These are all messages that what was is no longer up to the task of what's coming in for your biggest life.

You may find that your personal preferences change, sometimes dramatically. Maybe you used to like wearing a particular clothing style or color, and suddenly that no longer suits you. Or it could be that your favorite food used to be ice cream and now it's fresh vegetables. Sometimes it's even as light as changing your computer settings or favorite tv shows, or genre of books and movies.

A significant sign that you are ready to live a bigger life is when you start noticing your messages. You start seeing things in a different way, such as billboard signs speaking to you or the radio song singing to you. Maybe unusual sights pique your interest, like squirrels showing up to escort you as you take your morning walk. Maybe you take notice of people who you aren't naturally drawn to for some reason, and suddenly you see them in a different light. Or people are saying the same thing in different ways and at different times—you notice a thread, a message in their words.

Speaking of words, it could be that your language changes—both your inner and your outer voice changes vocabulary, tense, or subject choice. Your outer world is an expression of your inner world, so if your inner world is full of fear, your outer world will likely have all kinds of potential threats. If your inner world expects great things, your outer world will likely be offering them. Opportunities are attracted to you by your thoughts.

All opportunities are potential realities, waiting for you to choose to act on them. You don't really need to try to generate them because they will find you in magnetic attraction to your thoughts, beliefs, and being. Rather, they are yours to choose to pursue or not.

All these messages are measures of the degree of change for which you are making space to live your biggest life. Think of it like having a full closet—if it's already full, you have no place to put the new things you buy. You must make space in your closet to accommodate your new items. So, to the degree that things are breaking, not working, ending, and releasing is to the degree you can expect things to change in creating your biggest life yet.

Disguises that Bigger Messages Wear

Ironically, when things seem to be most chaotic or you feel the worst, you're actually getting ready to break through to a new life level. That's because you're highly aware of your 'symptoms' in an unavoidable way and you're out of your comfort zone. You're in the process of going past anything that you know already. In short, when you exceed your historical reference points, you no longer have safety, security, or stability in some way. And that feels like you've lost control.

It's hard to see the opportunity to grow because it is buried in the confusion, anxiety, frustration, overwhelm, anger, and even fear (amongst other states). Life moves fast and seems to be increasing in speed over time. The only way for you to navigate the complexities of modern living is to step into your personal opportunities to be your best by creating your own 'constants' amid the chaos of dynamic evolution. In other words, your understanding must go deeper to understand the Bigger Messages in your life to assign meaning to your experiences and give yourself stability from within.

DEFINING A 'BIGGER MESSAGE'

As a seeker of greater truth and meaning, you're on the leading edge of change. Despite the perceived obstacles in your life, you are continuing to reach out for transformation (or you wouldn't be reading this!). You know that the path to transformation is clarity through profound understanding of your experiences. Often feelings of potential (or actual) suffering are the guideposts to the fastest path of transformation.

Your life experiences—especially the ones that don't feel so good—lead you into your next best level in every moment. By acknowledging what's really happening, you give yourself the gift of sovereignty, or absolute personal decision-making (and, along with it, accountability). Know that the path to your best, boldest, and biggest life is through your life symptoms and situations. As of this moment, you can accept the hidden invitation and reframe seemingly negative situations in your mind to become the barometer measuring your shift towards your best life.

You can also prioritize the personal freedoms you want to experience in your life, which sometimes become evident by what you are not experiencing now. Essentially, there are four freedoms that successful people enjoy and that are available to you too.

1. **Time**—they have the time they want and need to do what they want and need to do, be, or have their best life
2. **Money**—they have financial freedom to support their life choices. They may or may not be 'wealthy'...but they have enough to feel comfortable and not stressed about cash flow.
3. **Being**—they have time to just 'be' in their lives. They can enjoy the present moment. They don't feel pressure to always be doing something for themselves or others. They can get up on any given morning and not feel rushed into any situation or circumstance because they have the latitude to simply 'be.' (Some say we are human beings, not human doings, right?)

4. **Choice**—this, I believe, is the most powerful force for change on the planet—choice. When you have the opportunity and ability to make choices in life, whatever area of life they are in, you are in your own flow. You are tuned in to your essential power. And you have the freedom to express your commitment to your own happiness by making choices.

Once you decide the type of freedom that is most important to you, you can focus on activities that allow you to make progress toward and enjoy it. Of course, these freedoms are not mutually exclusive; however, it can be easier to manifest them through prioritizing your attention and taking informed action based on your Bigger Messages.

Bonus: later in this book, we'll cover how to manifest what you really want, which is a nice complement to understanding which type(s) of freedom you want to experience more in your life.

A word about some typical challenges that can seem to block your success when you start acting on your Bigger Messages. Beginning with the word 'typical,' which is a complete misnomer because each person has unique variables, paradigms, and backstories. There is nothing 'typical' about challenges that show up in the real world because they all need to be addressed in some way.

With that in mind, there are two primary challenges that trip people up at their core. The first is 'I'm not worthy' (or I'm not 'enough') and the second is some version of 'I'm unlovable.' Typically, one of these two are really at the bottom of nearly every limitation, constriction, projection, assumption, and/or self-sabotaging thought. The good news is that once you make the commitment and create the internal shift required, you create new opportunities. Following are six variations on how those two basic challenges can wear masks in everyday life.

1. Old GPS:
As you've grown, you're still trying to navigate by old systems and paradigms of how the world is organized. It's like trying to fly a plane with a map from 1927—the terrain just isn't like that anymore! In practical terms, this looks like leaning on a learned coping strategy of being invisible for safety, nurturing others at your own expense, and/or having a 'lack' (or scarcity) mentality. Updating your GPS will support you in having a fresh perspective and creating what you really want in your life.

This is not a 'Guiding Profit System' that will work for you to become abundant—instead, discover what you can do to see your GPS with fresh perspective for new choices. Entrepreneuring isn't about fame and fortune first—those are natural by-products of doing what you love in the right way for others to appreciate and using the right manifestation formula for you. Figure out how you create freedom in your life and then teach it, so you'll be making a living from who you are! ;-)

2. Practical How-To's:
Sometimes the basics of living life—time management, navigating relationships, handling sticky situations—can trip people up. When you find yourself unable to make basic decisions about how to live your life every day—things that you know and handle all the time—it could be that a Bigger Message is trying to get your attention. Or you might find that your days are consumed in managing the minutiae of everyday living, so it feels like you are missing out on your best life as you manage details. When the practical how-to's either

become a mystery or confusing, or overwhelming, it's time to take a step back and see what is being masked by the minutiae.

3. Soul Song:

Being confused on what you're really here to do, what your gifts are, and how to make a meaningful difference in your life. There is an illusory container that limits living your soul song—and you can shatter it when you know how. When you limit your self-expression, it can reflect your low self-worth or feeling that you will be rejected for doing so. Birds don't care if their individual song is beautiful or makes sense... they are born to chirp and sing and so they do! Trees don't focus on being straight or linear or symmetrical... they simply grow as they are with the conditions they are in when seeded and over time. The same is true for people who align with their soul song and allow it to express fully.

At the same time, everything in modern society wants to ensure people conform, follow the rules, and check in with everybody else around defining appropriate behavior—all of which can stifle a soul song. When you're feeling like you have more to offer life, there is surely a Bigger Message waiting to be acknowledged.

4. The Big F:

The assorted fears that come up that become paralyzing, including fear of judgment, having to leave people behind when you grow, making a decision and then getting bored with it, feeling trapped in undesirable situations and more.

Then there are the deeper fears, such as fear of failure, fear of not being enough, fear of fitting in, fear of freaking out and more literally suck the life out of your momentum—that can really feel damaging. When you understand the invitation in the fear, you can turn it into a productive focus. What does that mean? Fear only shows up when

DEFINING A 'BIGGER MESSAGE'

you are in action, going beyond what is known, familiar, or expected. When you make a decision or take action to go beyond your comfort zone, you will likely feel fear; within that experience is an invitation that beckons you to grow into new capability in some way. That is the invitation in fear... the Bigger Message hidden within the apprehension, angst, or anxiety.

Oh—one more note on fear... when you move toward fear, it will shrink in proportion to your courage. Face the fear and step into new confidence which can magnetize new opportunities in all kinds of different ways.

5. Distortions:

The dysfunctional core beliefs that twist your clarity in making decisions and progress, like confusing consciousness with healing, the imposter phenomenon (if they really knew me, they'd know I don't know what I'm doing and leave me), approaching relationships with what you think they want vs. who you really are and how to see through them, are distortions. Sometimes distorted thinking is a result of other peoples' projections about who they think you should be vs. who you are... in that case, it is a matter of recognizing that it's not your distortion and releasing it.

One technique is to identify the projection or distortion, and simply 'return to sender' in your mind, like a gift that you don't want and choose to return. It doesn't hurt the sender; instead, it removes that pattern from your personal space, so you are clear to receive and then operate from your personal truth.

6. Self-Esteem:

To be more specific, LACK of self-esteem is a challenge that is all too common. Not being able to speak up about your abilities with confidence, not knowing you have something valuable to offer others, not being visible for your contributions and more will undermine your results. Learning how to access your natural inner self-confidence is a power approach to a better quality of life.

Discovering the Bigger Messages at work in your own life is the best way to create the life you really want to live.

Differences Can Surface Bigger Messages

One of the best ways to assess anything is to notice the difference, the contrast, between two states of being. For example, just as it's impossible to know what's hot if you don't know what cold feels like, it's challenging to know how your life is doing right now if you don't know that you can have something different. That contrast—that sensation of the difference between two ends of a continuum—is one of the Bigger Messages you can pay attention to right now to create your boldest life.

You can also get what you think you want and realize it's not what you thought it would be, so you need to learn and reassess going forward. Considering your contrast takes getting really honest with yourself—also a key to good living in general, by the way—because your inner wisdom never lies. Just as you'll get caught if you try to fool yourself into thinking your body won't notice polishing off that cake, your inner wisdom will know if you're lying to yourself.

Try it for yourself right now—tell yourself your name is George (unless your name actually *is* George, in which case pick another name!). Feel what that feels like in your body and you will likely notice something—your stomach feels funny, your palms sweat, your body leans backward, your neck gets tense, you might feel heavy or even some sort of pain...those are physiological symptoms showing you that your body is not agreeing with that statement. Try it again by telling yourself your real name and feel your body's messages. Typically, it will feel calm, stable, 'right'—because that is your truth. (Think of it as your body processing the message from the right, or intuitive, side of the brain—it bypasses the logical left side.)

The same technique can be applied to understanding your Bigger Messages in life. When you are telling yourself a story or are stuck in a loop that is not helpful to you, you will know it. Simply close your eyes, state what you think is true about a current situation, your life experiences or relationships, and then feel your body to show you where your contrast is in that statement.

Once you've connected with your inner wisdom as it is now, go back in your memory to recall a time when you were really happy. How did it feel? What did you like to do? Who did you think you were then? This awakens your body's cellular memory and may even help you feel better right now, in this moment.

Now, once you're ready to move on, project out to how your life would look and how you would feel if you understood the greater context of your life and were happy in living your boldest life. This could be 30 days from now, a year from now, five years from now ... where you are now is not a predictor of your future, so really envision your best life. What does it look like? What are you doing? What clarity do you have then that you're missing now? (And then write that down—that's a clue for you!)

You can also play out different scenarios in your mind to resolve a current situation and see how your inner wisdom would guide you. For example, if you have a friendship where there are communication challenges, you can envision several potential actions—asking questions, scheduling quality time together, confronting, sending an email, etc.—to see which one will yield the most positive pay-off for you.

The idea is that you can use finding your contrast between what is and what could be as a way to understand the Bigger Messages that are coming in through your current life experiences and how to take action that is congruent with them.

Four Elements for Living a Bigger Life

When you are not living in alignment with your personal truth, or something is trying to get your attention so you can live your best life, it can be uncomfortable. It doesn't feel good to wear shoes that are too small and even worse to live a life that's too small or doesn't fit you. When something doesn't feel good, that's about the circumstance and a Bigger Message vs. who you are in your essential self; that is, who you are is trying to emerge and is making whatever is 'not you' stand out in stark contrast.

You must let go of the smaller stuff to live your bigger life. There are really four elements that contribute to (or detract from) your biggest, boldest, most vital life experience. They are as follows.

1. Mental

Your mind is very powerful and what you believe is what will come true.

One story that demonstrates this is that of George Dantzig. Back in 1939, George was running late for class—he got there just in time to copy down two problems that he assumed were his homework.

Two days later, he turned it in to his professor. And shortly after that, he heard from his stunned professor—because George had just solved two of the problems considered 'unsolvable' by the mathematical greats for centuries! But George didn't know he wasn't supposed to solve the problems, so he did! And your mind is the same... what you believe is true is the #1 predictor of your ability to live your best life.

2. Emotional

Your emotions are the expression of the feelings your body experiences.

That is, you have feelings (prickly, clammy, expansive) which become emotions (jealous, uncomfortable, joyous). Think of it as E(nergy) in MOTION—E-MOTION. Literally, what you feel will be processed through your feeling filters until you have an awareness that you can consciously understand. How you interpret the world through your emotions (and mindset) determines your level of good health and vitality every day. As Wayne Dyer said, "Loving people live in a loving world. Hostile people live in a hostile world. Same world."

3. Spiritual

Your connection to the unseen through your intuition and/or higher power, whatever that might be for you, determines how much you trust what is happening in the world around you.

That is because your spiritual connection is a measure of the relationship you have with yourself. If you feel centered in your life, experience the joy that comes from knowing that you have a significant and unique purpose in the world, and surrender to what 'is' because of faith in something bigger than you, you are likely to be happier. And when you are happier, you are healthier and more magnetic to people and opportunities.

4. Physical

Your physical body is the container for the energy that is you on all these levels as well as the cumulative recording instrument of your life in motion.

Internationally-known spiritual teacher Caroline Myss says, "Your biography becomes your biology." And, unfortunately, that means your body—and your physical world—is the last place where symptoms can show up to be addressed. Your symptoms—in your body and in your life—are your guideposts to what needs to be addressed in your life to gain new freedom. When awareness expresses itself through the physical world, at that point, the only way out is through it.

When all four elements of your life synchronize well, life feels easy. When things are not syncing up so well, there is disharmony and dis-ease. The good news in that is every sting, every ping, every not-so-good-feeling situation is surfacing a Bigger Message for your consideration.

Perception Is Everything

Perception is your translation of what you see and experience in your world. For example, there is a humorous cartoon that shows a man on a deserted island with binoculars looking out at a boat coming to shore. That boat has a man with binoculars looking at the island. The first man is saying "Boat—I'm getting rescued!" and the second man is saying "Land—I'm getting rescued!" What you see from your point of view validates your belief systems.

When it comes to perception, you have learned from others about how to interpret the world around you. As a result, there are distortions, misidentifications, and duplicated imprints that dictate what you're doing by default instead of choosing in full presence in the 'now' moment. You simply think and do as you always have... and, over time, your perceptions will create paradigms, or fixed belief systems.

As another example, if you hold the puzzle pieces but don't have the puzzle box lid with the picture on it, you don't perceive that you have direction in life. Likewise, if you have the picture but don't have the individual pieces that it takes to make that complete image, you're also at a loss. Either way, humans are known for judging, or even tossing out, what we don't understand... which results in challenges that may be reinforced if you experience multiple situations without positive result.

If you find your life is stuck at the same level, even as you try new things and focus on growing your perception, it likely means your attention may be misplaced. You've probably been focused on getting by from a needs-based, or survival, place. Where we put our attention is what we create so if your attention is on getting through the tough times (without really understanding the Bigger Message), then you'll get more of that to reinforce that experience. Ironically, we humans like to know that we are right and, after all, if you feel bad or have life drama, there must be a good reason for it, right?

NO!

You don't want to look for evidence that you're right in thinking you can't live your best, most amazing life! Instead, you want to find evidence that you are ready to move forward with your life in new ways. (And, by now, you might already be seeing how that could be possible...) ;+)

If you find yourself in one of the following states, chances are your perception is distorted. Consider how each of the following statements may describe some part of your life right now.

1. **Discontent** where you aren't satisfied or at peace with what is in your life or how you're expressing your true self. When your life does not represent your truth, it doesn't feel good on multiple levels.
2. **Disconnect** from self, Source and others that becomes known by a sense of isolation, a desire to hibernate, a withdrawal from social connection that is about contraction rather than expansion into something deeper within.
3. **Disharmony** in how things are not quite fitting or coming together.
4. **Distress** as a form of anxiety that reflects your inner pain, sorrow, or misgivings about something happening in your life.
5. **Disease** as illness *or* dis-ease as resistance (in the form of not letting go of old beliefs, even though you know they don't serve you anymore, such as: needing to incessantly know more, staying in overwhelm, issues of self-confidence, the 'knowing it all' syndrome, not ready to do something, procrastination and/or over-preparation, etc.)

The good news is that understanding the Bigger Messages of your life will give you context, clarity, and new choices. By identifying what is causing the 'dis-'(content, connect, harmony, stress, or ease), you give yourself a place to start learning what you need to know. If you aren't quite sure which type of 'dis-' is being triggered, try to imagine various scenarios (so you don't need to physically experience them) so you can surface the feelings and explore what feels more aligned with your truth.

The Consequences of Taking Action

As you act on your Bigger Messages, there will be consequences. That's called the Law of Cause and Effect—for every action, there is a reaction equal to or even greater than the original action. Basically, you make things happen through action, meaning you create an outcome or consequence of doing something different. While your intention is always positive, you may discover unintended outcomes occur as well.

For example, you may get a Bigger Message that it's time to take your relationships more seriously. That can mean that you use greater discernment about who you allow in your world, and you are more aware of the quality of your relationships. You may find that long-time friends and acquaintances take you for granted or vice-versa, or that you don't choose your friends but, instead, receive them when they find you without considering whether that person belongs in your world. You may discover that you need to have difficult conversations, which could mean apologizing, teaching someone how to treat you, calling out an imbalance, or asking for a different type of relationship dynamic.

And that's just one example... every time you act on a Bigger Message, you open new possibilities that include both positive and 'shadow' options. Either way, the idea is that you will benefit from the Bigger Message in the end because it is tailored to you, your life's circumstances, and what you really want.

By the way, remember you are the only one who can determine whether a Bigger Message is relevant and meaningful to you. So, when you choose to act on a Bigger Message, your friends, family, and colleagues may judge you as being irrational or doing something so out of character that they try to talk you out of it. Their intention is to protect you but that urge also keeps you in their mental box of who they believe you to be...when you change, they likewise have to change and that can take a minute.

Acting on a Bigger Message can also surface other insights, like when you decide to show up more powerfully in your day-to-day life and you find out just how much you've been undervalued or have been playing small. Every step on the path of becoming more aware of your life dynamics and goals can yield unexpected clarity.

One of my mentors once told me that, once a person steps on the path of self-awareness, they can never get off it because they will know how much they don't know. For people who choose to 'sleep' through self-examination and ignore or avoid personal development, know they are doing the best they can with their goals in mind. You cannot change them; instead, you can change how you respond to them. Ideally, you extend them grace and compassion and allow them to have the life experience they are choosing.

That's a good point too...you cannot expect someone else to be different or to want more. Instead, you can model living a great life through proactive, positive change. And, if they ask, share with them what you are doing and how you are approaching your own process. Part of living a quality life is to not judge yourself or others or compare results. But it can be really easy to want *everyone* to find this new level of contentment and, so, tell everyone else what they should be doing.

One of my clients was so excited about the clarity he got from our work together that he went back into the office and told his colleagues what they should be doing...and he got pushback. Some people thought he was crazy, insensitive, and pushy because they did not ask for the insight or guidance and it was both unexpected and not necessarily relevant to their life.

I believe you can't say the wrong thing to the right people. In a, well, bigger sense, these people maybe did need to hear a new perspective. However, it was a bit painful for my client and it could have easily taken the jelly out of his donut if he took their reactions personally.

So, the consequences of acting on your Bigger Messages can create big waves in your relationships, cause unintended outcomes, and even yield other insights for your reflection.

How Relationships Work with Bigger Messages

Since we touched on relationships, let's keep going because relationships are pivotal in receiving and acting on Bigger Messages.

It is through our relationships with others that we learn the most, which is always for our betterment even when it doesn't feel like it. One of my clients 'got' that she should have a talk with her husband about their future. She wasn't feeling as connected with him as when they were first married and now, a decade later, felt like they were more roommates than spouses. She acted on that Bigger Message through symbolism; she got a crystal—symbolizing clarity—and placed it in their bedroom. She thought nothing more of it beyond her intention for facilitating new clarity between them.

That evening, after dinner and the kids were in bed, her husband surprisingly initiated a conversation. He confessed he had been having an affair for several months because he was unhappy. While he ended the affair that day, he also felt their marriage had come to an end. Obviously, this was not the clarity my client was looking for... and, at the same time, once the divorce was finalized and the dust settled, they each found their new partner, re-married, and became better co-parents. The last I heard, my client was living in Hawaii and happier than ever. A Bigger Message can bring unwanted insights that can lead to unforeseen rewards.

But what if you get a Bigger Message that encourages you to do something that can affect your family, like move to a new country? What if you get a Bigger Message that says you need to focus on your health and that takes away from your availability with friends? What if you get a Bigger Message that encourages a significant financial investment, and your resources are tied up in a mutual account with someone else?

In any case where others are affected by what you have learned through a Bigger Message, remember there are different ways to accomplish any outcome. Maybe you can find a way to work and travel in that new country, or you invite your friends to join you in working out or attending cooking healthy workshops, or you start a side business to get the funds together on your own... in all cases, you have free will to decide how you want to interpret and act on the Bigger Message. If what you perceive or do yields unexpected results, simply ask to receive a next level clarifying Bigger Message.

Life has a way of bringing you what you need to grow. You have multiple daily opportunities to receive fresh insights and take new action. Part of the process includes determining the potential impact on others as you go—what's the trade-off if you do A, B, or C? Only you can decide if that trade-off is acceptable or not. And only you can decide how you want to grow through your Bigger Messages. What gets interesting is that others will also get to grow through your

Bigger Messages...just ask any parent how they felt when their child announced a life change for the first time or any entrepreneur who got pushback from making an unexpected business decision. People will be affected by what you choose to do . . . and then they get to decide how they want to act on their part of the situation.

There is a pattern for Bigger Messages that can be helpful . . . we will get into that next.

The Bigger Message Formula

There is a clear pattern for considering how to determine where to start creating your bigger life through understanding the context and the substance of what is happening in your life. When people stumble onto this pattern, it feels like magic—because things seem to open in a nearly effortless way. They get the messages, teachings, or clarity quickly and easily and are able to apply them to get to their next level—almost like graduation from one grade to the next.

This pattern is both unique and universal at the same time. By looking at your own life using a universal 'filter,' it is possible to understand a much larger context with all the potential possibilities within it. That is, drawing on universal principles to have the largest perspective possible for viewing an individual life in the moment gives a unique snapshot of what is right now along with the mystery of what could be from that point forward. It is unique to the individual but is universal in both possibility and consequence in relation to others (who are all, incidentally, individuals having their own universal experience!).

For example, the things that irk you most, or that you judge most frequently, are often patterns that you have experienced or even created in your own life. Think your friend numbs herself out to her relationships with too much shopping/alcohol/social drama? Where are you numbing out in your life? Think your cousin needs to settle down and focus to have a better life? Where are you holding yourself back or playing small? This kind of mirroring can be informative when you can remain an objective observer of the pattern vs. the critic that wants to play a blame game. Blame, shame, guilt, or pointing fingers is not helpful for anyone and generally will not get you a positive result. But noticing where you experience patterns can literally change your life.

This is the core of the Bigger Message—looking at your own life through the objective 'lens' of universal laws and principles to understand where there is disconnect from what is and what you want. The goal is to close the gap between where you are and where you want to be by creating intentional change through informed choices and focused action.

It's important to remember an ages-old truism as you begin to see and translate the Bigger Messages of your life into fresh results. Einstein noted that "the same thinking that created the problem cannot solve it." While the seeds of the solution are in the message, it is still necessary to add your interpretation or perspective to gain clarity. That means you'll need to stop the normal brain 'chatter' to get new ideas. And just because you may not have been able to do that on your own doesn't mean that you are wrong—it means you are human, and you just haven't learned what you need to know yet!

So, here is the Bigger Message formula:

$$\frac{\text{New Choice + Focused Action =}}{\text{New Conscious Results for Bigger Life}}$$

$$\text{Instigating Event + Clarity = Bigger Message}$$

(As in, read this formula as a mathematical formula—the top lines are 'over' the second, or below, line.)

In other words, the Bigger Message is derived by considering a triggering event that requires clarity. That underlies any new results you experience in your life. Once you perceive the Bigger Message, you give yourself new choices from which to act which results in consciously creating and living your bigger life.

Sounds simple, right? However, when you really look at what's happening in each of these areas, you can discover some complex and amazing insights about yourself. Let's explore the formula in action.

Cues and Clues

The main thing to remember is that each area of your life contains cues and clues about what is happening for you, and each message in one area of your life has an impact on the others. For example, consider the following life areas: self-care, career, family, personal wisdom, spirituality, wealth, reputation, health, significant other relationship, creativity, intellectual challenge, friends, and community . . . living more fully into each of these life areas becomes more efficient when you receive and understand your messages.

One of the more common insights many people have is the discovery that they've been trying to model up until now a particular system of being (participating with, learning from, being 'cool,' etc.) that doesn't really work for them. For many people, these ways of being come from how they are raised; we are socialized from our connection with authority figures, teachers, peers, and even popular media like sitcoms or movies. It's perfectly natural to try on new or different ways of being, given that humans are social creatures; however, the whole point of life is to find one's *own* way of being. And that's the flexibility that is afforded by seeing your life through the lens of Bigger Messages. You learn your own style and way of being in the world in a larger, more expansive way.

The Bigger Message is about seeing what's happening with the most open viewpoint possible while still giving structure so that you can take it and make it work for creating your biggest life. The formula is designed to give you clarity about how to see and interpret your greater truths and make new choices to get to your next best level faster and easier. It's about creating success by your own interpretation and definition. That is, after all, what you, and only you, are accountable for—your result.

Therefore, the Bigger Message applies to every area in your life and will likely show up in multiple ways. The idea is to understand the Bigger Message in one area of your life to positively influence your other life areas. Each life area message weaves in and out and through the others but they stand on their own as well. There is a saying that "how you do anything is how you do everything"; the idea is that you can see what you are doing in at least one life area to create a more intentional action plan. You must get past where you are to live bigger...you must get new insights by having fresh awareness. And that is entirely possible when you understand how to use your Bigger Messages for decision-making.

Let's make this more concrete by considering the story of Marie* (name changed for the purpose of sharing here), who at age 50 found herself unhappy yet again after seemingly changing her whole life. She had been generally unhappy, living in a small apartment for many years, tolerating a stagnant relationship, in a going-nowhere job where she felt unappreciated for her true talents and was not making enough money. She decided to geographically move her life and rent a home that was somewhat out of her budget but affordable if she cut back on extras. She started a new job and took a break from the ten-year relationship that didn't offer any future.

Within six months, she discovered she mostly liked her new home, but wasn't sure about the new locale. She went back to the dysfunctional relationship (with distance now being a factor) and didn't like her new job as she felt not only underappreciated by her colleagues but under attack for her femininity and, adding insult to injury, still wasn't making enough money. (Incidentally, upon doing her taxes the first year after her move, she realized that she made $92,000 that year but was unaware of it and had nothing to show for it.) It seemed she was in pretty much the same place even after apparently changing everything, and she needed help to see what happened.

Upon questioning, she admitted that her family had assigned her to the 'pretty baby doll' role, the beauty of her youth was a way to earn money as an exotic dancer, and she had turned to substances to numb herself from the attention of unsavory men. She never expected to be able to earn a living through her intelligence, skills, and talents because she was 'pretty' (vs. being 'smart enough') but had gone to college because she needed to prove something to herself. Can you see the messages in her life? She couldn't.

The Bigger Messages for Marie were around the following:

- Deserving the money that she earned from her intelligence and talents.
- Having a significant relationship that honored all of her being (not just physical).
- Living and working in supportive and healthy environments.
- Cultivating her own innate talent and skills.
- Loving her beauty from the inside out.
- Honoring, accounting for, and being in gratitude for the money she did earn.
- Accepting all of who she knew herself to be now (versus who others said or thought she was) without seeking external validation from anybody else.

These are Bigger Messages that literally took her fifty years to recognize. She had multiple versions of the same instigating event and invitation for clarity. Could Marie have done it faster? Maybe. However, if she could have done it faster, she would not have experienced the depth of her messages.

In growth, there is always some pain involved, because what 'was' had to essentially die to allow the birthing energy to begin. Had Marie not experienced the range of messages that she did in a repetitive way, her life would be a different story and her messages would have shown up differently. We're always exactly where we need to be to receive our Bigger Messages and we recognize them when we're ready. (The key is to cultivate your readiness to receive the message, as the message will guide you once you 'get' it.)

To continue the story of Marie, she entered into a relationship with the man of her dreams; however, her job was never satisfying—she quit a year later under conditions of deep harassment and multiple projections of where she was deficit. She suffered from post-traumatic stress disorder. The man of her dreams turned out to be emotionally immature and abusive. She became depressed and suicidal. And so, she picked up and moved nearly ten hours away to get a fresh start. She met another man, with whom she has shared a challenging relationship that mirrors her previous ones.

She has yet to find worthwhile employment despite her degrees and unique talents, which is showing her it's time to become a leader in her field through self-employment. And she has continued to look for validation that her worldview 'as is' is right by replaying old scenarios. Until she sees her Bigger Messages with clarity, her choices are limited, and her actions remain in the purview of what she already knows. Her circumstances change but she recreates the same outcomes. (While we'll continue to reflect on Marie's experience as a rich case study, know that there is a happy ending—she eventually did find the man of her dreams and is currently happier than she's ever been with her life.)

If you recognize yourself in Marie's story, then it's time to get new clarity about the Bigger Messages of your life so you can make some new choices. It's your choice as to what life area you want to begin with . . . you may decide to start with whatever comes up at first glance, with a particular challenging situation happening now or go all the way back to explore how each life area has shown up and progressed through your life.

The value in considering it from a longer time vantage point is that you can look for the source of your pattern over time. You aren't merely looking at current results, or symptoms, but the root causes of your world. You can look sequentially at that one issue/pattern at a time, or chronologically at what patterns have presented in a given timeframe to discover their current state of resolution. Regardless of your approach, you're looking at your life with new objectivity because you're searching for the Bigger Messages.

It's All Connected

> *"You don't have to go back and deal with childhood issues, because those childhood issues produced a vibration within you that you are still offering—which is producing today issues. You can shift your vibration a whole lot easier when you're dealing with today issues, than trying to deal with childhood issues. It's the same vibration. That vibration that was creating childhood issues, now it's creating today issues."*
>
> ~ Abraham-Hicks

The bottom line is that everything is connected—everything. That's another aspect of the Bigger Message. That means what you do in the details of your day affects the outcomes in your life. How you look at your life and what you believe in and how you show up determines your results. The instigating event offers you the opportunity for clarity through understanding a Bigger Message. Once you have your message, you have new choices available for you to take new action that will, ideally, lead to your biggest life. It's all connected.

To know that for yourself, take a moment and look around your world right now. The chair you're sitting in might be part of a set, it is comprised of various material components that come from different sources, it was made by someone somewhere in the world based on a design that someone else created, and each of them have families who support an economy... you get the idea—and that's just the chair!

Another example is the story of Joshua Chamberlain, a 34-year-old professor of modern languages, without whom life in the U.S. would be very different. In fact, it wouldn't be the United States—it would be a combination of districts, states, and countries. It was Chamberlain who was the reluctant commander of the Union Army at Gettysburg by virtue of surviving the battle when his superiors were killed. The Union Army had started with more than 1,600 men and, after losing ground five times, having no ammunition and only 80 men left to defend against the ever-growing Confederate Army. It was a desperate moment when all other options had been exhausted.

Chamberlain decided to do the unthinkable—he ordered the 80 ragged survivors to get their bayonets and unexpectedly, in a one-time go-for-broke move, charge at the Confederate Army. The Confederates were so surprised that they figured surely there were more soldiers in the Union Army than they'd seen and so surrendered. It was the deciding battle of the Civil War and, because of Joshua

Chamberlain not knowing what else to do, the U.S. became forged into the cultural tableau and world super-power of today. It's all connected through time, space, and humanity.

Speaking of humanity, you are here because you are standing on the shoulders of your ancestors. For better or worse, your lineage has brought you to this point in history to live your biggest life—one that they likely could not even dream of during their lifetime. When you really stop for the first time to consider how interwoven your world is with the rest of a much bigger world, it is mind-boggling.

To bring it back to your current reality, whatever you're experiencing in your life reflects the bigger picture. Much like the proverbial tip of the iceberg, life's greatest opportunities lie in what is not visible to us. In fact, it is often because it is not visible to us that we know it is our next message. Like the wind, we cannot see it, but we know where it's been by the trees blowing, leaves rattling, grass flattening. Your Bigger Message may be disguised but it is there, and you know it because you can see where it's been in your life through your instigating event.

Others around you may not understand what you're going through because they don't need that message, which is all the more frustrating when you're in the middle of trying to figure out a message. It's always much easier to see other people's Bigger Messages than our own because we aren't standing in our own shadow, with our blind spot blocking us, to see them (and the same is true for others who are looking in from the outside). When other people don't understand why you're stuck on something seemingly so evident, it is a sign that you're really in the middle of a significant transition.

In the throes of decoding intense messages, it is important to understand that there is a greater truth behind whatever it is that seems to be causing you difficulty. Sometimes the greater truth can be discovered quickly, if you simply stop to consider what that could be; other times, it is more elusive and a longer discovery process. Greater truths are based on universal principles but are unique in how they manifest in each person's life. Remember that your greater truths are for you, not for anyone else, and vice-versa.

Principles of The Bigger Message

Following are some different ways to consider and see the unchanging principles of the Bigger Message(s) within your current situation.

A Bigger Message will show up time and time again if it is not recognized or acknowledged (like Marie!). Consider it as a thread that runs through several different types of situations or experiences, or maybe even through your whole life. It is something that shows up again and again, creating a pattern over time.

As a mental exercise, look at your own life as a giant tapestry. From the front, you can see the beautiful colors and intricate patterns that are unique to you. From the back, you see all the unfinished threads, the unsightly knots, the places it wants to unravel. If you pulled on any one of those threads to try to make the back more visually pleasing, you would unravel what makes the front so beautiful. It is because of the individual threads that the pattern is beautiful. If you don't like the pattern, or greater truth, you are seeing in your own life, you can change it but you must see it first. Once you weave the loose ends into the greater piece, the tapestry becomes smoother, more complete, with a richer aesthetic overall.

Your experiences, or Bigger Messages, show up over time and will create patterns to help you make sense of your world. These patterns create a frame of reference to create order around what you experience. Understanding your reference points will point the way to your greater truths.

For example, to reference Marie's story, her inaccurate reference point was that her physical beauty was the only thing of value about her. With any beautiful woman, we know that this is simply not true, because her outer beauty only scratches the surface of her true inner beauty. This reference point created a whole pattern for her in not being recognized for her contributions at work. She responded to being recognized for her looks but judged herself as 'too pretty' to be professionally competent; in her mind, beautiful women could not be taken seriously. She was not being paid enough because she felt put off to the side as others got raises, never feeling 'smart enough' to be a real player in management, and felt awkward when applauded for her skills.

This inner incongruence and inability to see herself as valuable beyond her appearance was also her reference point for creating relationships that couldn't give her true sustenance, in how she related to women professionally and personally, and in using various substances to numb her intuitive sensitivities from unscrupulous men attracted to her superficially but from who she received validation for what her family seemed to prize most about her. All from one reference point because she missed the Bigger Message about the truth of her inner worth and beauty. What's your reference point? What messages might you be missing?

Results also demonstrate your Bigger Messages. That is, where you are now is a result of the decisions and choices you made in your past based on what you knew then. Those decisions and choices were the best you could make at the time, given your resources and awareness at the time. Your current results give you a key as to where your Bigger Messages can make the biggest difference.

If we consider Marie's results, we see that she moved to new locales but held on to old relationship patterns despite the dysfunction and lack of future. All she changed was the venue.

As Jon Kabat-Zinn says, "wherever you go, there you are." Marie felt unfulfilled, with a vague sense of something better but clinging to the crumbs of what good she gleaned from analyzing and reframing what was in the relationship. She paid homage to the history, and desperately tried to see the positive in this man who was contributing only a minimal amount of time and effort to their relationship. Her result showed that she wasn't getting what she wanted in a relationship. Her internal reference reinforced that she didn't believe she deserved it because she was only a pretty face.

Another factor in being aware of Bigger Messages in your life is the significance of what you are doing—the significance of the impact of knowing and applying the wisdom of your Bigger Message. Are you making a difference? Is being aware of the Bigger Message going to make a significant difference in how you create your world?

For Marie, she was working in higher-level corporate positions, and changed jobs four times in five years. The significance of her contribution was undervalued, but she didn't realize it was because she undervalued it. She was doing her work because of being expected to do it as a job rather than doing her work out of the passion and true talent that was the motivator for her to get into her field of work. It was a case of performance versus true contribution. And when she did change jobs, she consistently created more of what she wanted, but didn't recognize her success in doing so. She continued to find reasons to be disillusioned because she couldn't see the significance of her true gifts and contribution.

When presented with ideas on how to be a voice for her passion as an industry avant-garde leader, she couldn't comprehend how that could be possible, much less her true purpose. These were her instigating events to invite greater clarity for conscious results for her best life. Her Bigger Message is that she couldn't see her own significance.

Remember, here is the Bigger Message formula:

New Choice + Focused Action = New Conscious Results for Bigger Life

---

Instigating Event + Clarity = Bigger Message

You must consider the instigating event until you have new clarity, which results in understanding the Bigger Message available to you. Your Bigger Message underlies your ability to create new results. Once you know your Bigger Message, you can see new choices and take new action that directly and proportionately leads to your best, bigger life.

The good news is that, like Marie, if you don't understand your instigating events and decode your Bigger Messages, you'll get another chance—they will continue to show up again and again until you get your clarity. Our collective purpose here is to learn, to work with our messages, and to understand consciously what we are creating. If we ignore, deny, neglect, or avoid this responsibility, it will present itself another time, another way, and usually in a bigger, louder way in order to get our attention. It is up to us to get through all the noise and distractions to get to our clarity so we can live our biggest life.

There can be moments where it feels like you have Bigger Messages that conflict, such as your awareness that you are a valuable being and your awareness that you need to earn a living despite feeling undervalued at the moment. However, with reflection, you can see that the Bigger Message at work is the one that says you are valuable because it is the one that will bring you to your best and greatest good in the long run. A Bigger Message is positive, personal, and yet based on universal principles, withstands the test of time, is simple, and just feels right.

You may be aware of the Bigger Messages in the lives of people around you. If that is the case, you can see them because you have a matching picture with them on that truth. Oftentimes, that means you have handled it for yourself, but it may be a mirror for you to see it more clearly. For example, if you notice that people are consistently late in meeting or calling you as previously agreed, look at the value of time in your own life. Are you valuing time the way you have agreed to with yourself and others?

And, by the way, just because you see it doesn't mean you should share the Bigger Message with the other person—they may not be able to hear it yet. In a case like this, the only outcome would be risking the quality of that connection. Taking that further, you might not be close enough to them when that person is ready to receive their Bigger Message—which is when they would really benefit from your wisdom—to help them land it.

Once you understand the Bigger Messages at work in your life, having passed through the growth period that helped you receive them, you are free to apply what you've learned and move on. However, there may—and hopefully will—be new Bigger Messages that give you the opportunity to understand the context and substance of your life. If you get to a point where you understand all your Bigger Messages, you probably no longer need to be on this physical plane for a physical experience.

Now, that doesn't mean you learn and then die; instead, you can choose to stay on this physical plane and enjoy your newfound still point with the universe (although, at some point, the inevitable transition will occur). Some would say that, when reaching your still point—or profound contentment that is synchronized with universal rhythms—you have achieved enlightenment.

There are various definitions of what enlightenment means . . . being able to hold two opposing thoughts in your mind at the same time, stripping away all that is conditioned socialization and not-self, transcending physical concerns on command ... all of them, essentially, reference the inner self being in union with the greater consciousness. With that connection vibrant and foremost, a lot of the painful details of physical life no longer hold enough importance to create an emotional charge. After all, when you are a millionaire, does chasing pocket change seem like a good investment of your energy?

By reviewing your life through the lens of your Bigger Message discovery and decoding process, you'll likely see that what used to confound you is now just a part of who you know yourself to be; that is, if an instigating event were to occur for a Bigger Message that you've already experienced, it no longer presents the challenge it did at one time. There are some who would say that alone is what determines 'enlightenment'—the ability to handle what would have thrown you off at a previous time in your life. And once you know how to interpret that Bigger Message, it is no longer necessary for it to present in your life... *you got it.*

What To Do in the Middle of a Message

Life has a way of bringing you Bigger Messages in unexpected ways and timing. It's hard to remember that things are happening to show you a greater truth when you just have to fix your flat tire, move to a new house in the next 30 days or your significant other just said something hurtful. When you're in the middle of getting a message, you are essentially being 'activated' to that potential new awareness available through the Bigger Message behind the circumstance. And it may be accompanied by fear.

Physiologically, the body's response to fear is to stay small and quiet, to limit movement and breath, to contract in a waiting stance to defend against the perceived enemy. When you're in contraction, you're expanding your input data by focusing very narrowly on the alert signals you'll notice. That's why when you're in a reactive state that goes beyond your initial response, it will feel even more chaotic, dramatic, and destabilizing—there's too much input and your linear mind is trying to sort through historical data as well as present time. In that moment, it's best to do what you need to do to handle the urgency of the situation and, if possible, observe your thoughts so you can revisit them later to cull your Bigger Messages. In the moment, you may not be able to access your mind enough to notice your thoughts. Afterward, or as a general life response, you can mentally process your fear.

Generally, fear can be categorized into a few 'buckets.' Author Napoleon Hill lists six types of fear:

1. Fear of Poverty
2. Fear of Criticism
3. Fear of Ill Health
4. Fear of Loss of Love
5. Fear of Old Age
6. Fear of Death

When you fear a Bigger Message, particularly around one of these six core fears, ask yourself: "What's the worst that could happen?" Then proceed to actively answer it by putting it all out there—the absolute worst-case scenario. Use this new understanding of your fear to overcome it. Fear is a state of mind, and you control your state of mind; your mind is your servant.

For example, if you have an opportunity to share your message by speaking to 1,000 people at a conference and you're terrified you'll make a fool of yourself somehow, then that's the worst-case scenario, right? You could trip on your way to the stage, fumble your notes, stumble over your words, forget what you're talking about and, altogether, be completely ineffective and heckled off the stage.

Now consider the other side of that situation—ask "What's the best that could happen?" You could give a great presentation, inspire people to take new action, win over the crowd, and get new speaking gigs! When you focus on the positive and take action accordingly, fear has no place to take a foothold in your psyche.

However, as shared previously, if you find you are in an 'activated' state (fear, anger, anxiety, etc.), the most important thing you can do is to remain centered in what's happening without judgment, resistance, worry, doubt, or apathy. Each of these reactions will block or slow your ability to receive the Bigger Message in that moment. And these reactions can cause a sense of 'lack,' which can trigger all kinds of layered responses on top of your initial experience, keeping you in a contracted fear state.

So when you are in the middle of receiving, acting on, or experiencing the aftermath of a Bigger Message, especially one that is uncomfortable or feels like it's coming out of nowhere, the best thing you can do is observe what's happening and allow a sense of flow.

That means feeling your feelings fully, whatever they are, without judgment and emotionally surfing the feelings as they arise. This is not always so simple because we are socialized to just 'suck it up' or 'get through it' or 'buckle down and ride it out.' In all cases, any suppressed or repressed emotional response to what's happening gets, essentially, stuffed down in your physiology; over time, that can cause other challenges, including physical symptoms or an emotional landmine that goes off later in a seemingly unrelated event.

It is also possible to want to prolong a happy experience in the middle of a Bigger Message pivot. Albert Einstein recommended we measure time in relative terms; his example was something like sitting next to someone attractive is never long enough but touching a hot stove seems like forever. That means that all experiences are actually fleeting; it's when we try to force them to push through quickly or remain in a prolonged state that sends the experience sideways. By allowing the experience to unfold, the Universe has wiggle room to bring you the optimal experience for you.

Getting Intentional Messages

Once you're through the most immediate part of the situation, you can review what happened in order to understand your Bigger Messages.

For example, if you had an argument with your best friend that now seems not worth your reaction at the time, it's likely that a past memory was triggered by the current conversation. It might be that you are being invited to speak your truth, ask for what you want, or let down your guard in order to become closer. You might also discover that the relationship has really run its course and it's time to move on. In any case, it's less about your friend and more about your Bigger Message as an indicator of how to move forward in living your best life.

Living from the truth of your Bigger Messages happens on two levels—one being the current moment to choose how you move forward and the other being about interpreting what happened in the past as a contributing element to the present circumstance. Either way, inviting the clarity afforded by understanding your Bigger Messages is a process of intentional change. When you have a way to practice proactive growth, you are no longer at the mercy of whatever happens but are, instead, charting your course of life mastery through transformation.

One situation in which you might find yourself receiving a message is when you are in a perpetual state of upset about something—that is a significant sign that you're hiding from your truth. So the question becomes: what are you hiding from? The reality is that, when you become aware of that which you're hiding from, it no longer has negative power over any part of your experience. The answer to that single question will be your Bigger Message.

To identify additional messages for yourself when you are not currently activated, ask yourself the following questions:

- Am I complaining about someone or something?
- Am I blaming someone or something?

- Has a boundary been breached? Did I not enforce or honor it?
- Am I self-medicating or numbing out (escaping to movies, watching too much tv, using substances or alcohol, overeating, etc.) to avoid thinking/feeling something?
- Am I annoyed by someone or something? Irritated? Cranky?
- Am I avoiding someone/something? Procrastinating? Feeling under-prepared?

These questions allow you to dig beneath the superficial face of the current situation to do what is commonly called 'the work'; that is, you have to understand what's really happening—your Bigger Message—so you can address it at its source, the only solution for sustainable change.

Following are some of the most common situations that indicate Bigger Messages are trying to come to you.

1. Feeling rejected, betrayed, or abandoned; not 'belonging'; feeling alone, 'outside' or misunderstood
2. Avoiding action to avoid making mistakes from the need to be perfect; stuck in 'analysis paralysis'
3. Being ridiculed, mocked, or criticized; afraid of being a target for 'bad things' to happen (again)
4. Feeling like 'it' is too big to do or that you're not enough to do 'it'
5. Fearing the unknown; being destabilized when you don't know what will happen
6. Not believing in self; judging self for being who you are; having a vision in your head about you or your life that can be impossible to match
7. Worrying about what others say but seeking that validation anyway

8. Focusing on the 'what ifs'—what if I'm not happy, fail anyway, don't have excuses to fall back on, etc. —which keep you out of the present moment and thinking about things that may never actually occur

It's all too easy to allow the 'masks' of humanity to hide your Bigger Messages: busyness, judgment, scarcity, fear, distraction, focusing on others, needing everything to be perfect before taking action, etc. Beyond that, there are 'negative' emotions, such as anger, blame, shame, guilt, etc., that indicate our needs have not been met and that we are socially conditioned to process externally rather than go within, which is where it's possible to identify and integrate our Bigger Messages.

When you engage in a process of intentional self-discovery, you may feel doubt, question your thoughts, or feel that you don't know enough to get your messages. One way to support yourself through the process is to begin by writing out your intentions for what you would like to know as a result of your process. Then write out one question at a time, wait for clarity to come to you and write down what comes to you.

If you don't receive a message from that particular question, simply repeat the opportunity by asking another question and inviting clarity. Once you receive your Bigger Messages, you are at a choice point of whether to assimilate them into your life (or not). If you choose to apply the wisdom of the Bigger Message into your life, review the messages you've received and then break them down into what needs to happen in your life to assimilate and activate their power for transformation—this creates your action plan.

For example, here is a sample that demonstrates this process:

Intention: I want to know why I can't get ahead in my career.

Questions:

- Why didn't I get the promotion? Because it would have kept me in the company—I would be happier, and I wouldn't think about new options.
- Why don't I make more money? Because I'm in the wrong job in the wrong industry. I don't really care about what I do—it's just a paycheck anyway.
- Why am I so unhappy when I think about going to work? Because it's time for me to do what I really love.

In this case, the person who wants to get ahead in their career would see they are actually in a job that is keeping them small. If they want to be happy in their career, they are going to have to figure out what they really want to do and take action accordingly to get a new job or maybe even start a business. That could include taking classes to develop their skill set, networking with people to make new connections, or brushing up their resume.

Apply this same kind of thinking to any question or scenario you want to decode in your own life to see what presents.

Six Signs of Not Listening

Your Bigger Messages are always available; however, even knowing that there is something trying to get your attention, you may not be listening to your Bigger Messages. To make it easier for you to identify and focus on listening better, following are six signs that can signal you are not listening to your Bigger Messages.

1. You are repeating patterns—you're not letting go of what was and are stuck in re-living the message until you get it. (Think *Groundhog Day*, the movie that keeps Bill Murray trapped in personal time.)

The longer you go on repeating the pattern, the more embedded it becomes in your belief system and more power it has in taking over your free will. Why? Because the longer you act in the same way, the more likely you are to become unconscious about it as a habit. The key is to see where you are repeating patterns and decide consciously if that's a helpful pattern. For example, you might have a pattern of taking a morning break for a protein shake... or you might take a break with coffee and donuts. Both are patterns but which serves you best?

Here is another common pattern... dating the same person over and over again with different names. Many of my clients want to know what that's all about, although many are not happy to hear the answer. ;+)

Amazingly enough, the answer to dating the same 'person' is found in your own integrity because you are attracting the partners who match your energy signature. In other words, you are attracting that which matches your own frequency. When you upgrade your frequency (your energy field), you attract a higher-quality partner (and vice-versa). This means there is a natural congruence, or alignment, based on your own energy between you and another person.

If you want a different type of partner to show up for you, it's time to get into integrity with who you are and that which you want to experience. The Bigger Message is that when you *are* it, you will *attract* it.

2. You are living behind shields (addiction, perfection, obsession, substances, etc.) that keep you disassociated from living your boldest life. This is about trying to protect yourself from previous trauma that is getting triggered in your life today. Anything that numbs you from feeling pain or processing feelings you don't want to deal with can set the stage for putting up shields. Ironically, the shields keep you inside your walls vs. keeping others out. When you give your power to a shield, you become more vulnerable because you are not in control at that point. And, too often, we have heard stories of unscrupulous people taking advantage of people who are trying to protect themselves with some variety of a shield.

3. You tell your story over and over to anyone who will listen, believing it and living from it when that is your history rather than your future. The reason you might be doing this is because you're looking for validation or a different outcome to what happened in your past, or you might be trying to pull forward a peak experience into your now. Either way, life is meant to be lived in the present moment so watch yourself when recounting memories. There may be an invitation to release your attachment to what was so you can live into today more fully.

4. You experience interpersonal conflicts that seem familiar (i.e., have the same arguments with the same kinds of people, even if they are different people). Conflict happens when boundaries are being breached, when something or someone is not serving your highest good (or vice versa), or when you are missing information. The thread here is that if you are having the same types of conflicts repeatedly, there is a Bigger Message inviting you to lean in and listen so you can transcend the need for those conflicts.

5. You have physical illness or injury as your body tries to slow you down to get your Bigger Message. While you are busy living at the speed of modern life, your body has a deeper wisdom that paces natural rhythms. When your body realizes it's time for a break, it will find a way to make it happen. While it can be uncomfortable, painful, and frustrating, such a situation is prime fodder for tuning in and receiving a Bigger Message.

6. You sabotage your momentum; in other words, you manufacture your own 'speed bumps' and bang into walls rather than move forward with the energy of your Bigger Message guiding you. This one is self-explanatory and very likely one you have experienced at some point in your life. Did you get passed over for a promotion because you started uncharacteristically running late or dropping the ball on projects? Did you decide to start speeding just as you passed a police station? These are obvious examples, but it can be more subtle. Maybe you have an important meeting or public appearance, so you go for a new haircut and find your hair is too short/the wrong color/not flattering. Or maybe you get 90 percent through a project only to stutter for the last ten percent... and maybe don't complete the project at all. Where there is self-sabotage, there is opportunity through a Bigger Message.

When you are experiencing any one of these signs, it's likely you either aren't prepared for the changes that will occur in your life when you acknowledge your Bigger Messages, or you don't know how to handle them. Ironically, that's the very thing that will keep you from living your boldest life because, whether consciously or not, you're more committed to a perception of safety than of embodying your life transformation.

To set yourself up to hear your Bigger Messages more consistently, it's important to build your personal resilience. Savor your accomplishments, trust that your best life is yet to come, and release attachment to what your messages (and your life) should look like to avoid feeling the need to justify what happens next.

Remember you are in charge of creating your life and that you always have choices—there is no need to fear your Bigger Messages. You can take small, inspired steps toward incorporating your messages into your life. Find joy in discovering your Bigger Messages as the antidote to feeling fear (fear and joy cannot co-exist at the same time just as light and dark cannot be in the exact same place at one time).

Lastly, reframe tough situations in a way that acknowledges the growth opportunity being afforded through your understanding of the Bigger Message (even if you're not quite sure what that is yet).

For example, one of my twenty-something clients was upset that her father had been consistently absent in her youth and, when he was there, he was volatile and unpredictable in his disciplinary practices with her. She was going to call him and let him have it (again) for being a terrible father. However, by talking it through, she realized that growing through that experience gave her independence, the ability to speak her truth, and claim her personal power regardless of outer circumstances.

As a result, she decided to forgive him, so she didn't have to carry the poison and, even more, show him compassion. She recognized that no father intends to be a 'bad' father; instead, he himself had issues to be resolved. Today they have built a relationship based on candor, honesty, and respect. By reframing the tough situations, you find the gift of the Bigger Message in seemingly negative situations; you distill the positive juice from it to improve your options and opportunities.

Now, even if you KNOW you want to change your life and you know what you need to do, there may be times you can't follow through to make it happen. What's that about?

When you choose to create a result that is different from what you've already experienced, you are pushing beyond your comfort zone. Your comfort zone is what you have already determined is safe and secure—even if it's not what you really want.

For example, you may want to drop some weight—but you live in a colder climate and your body holds on to the weight for protection against the elements. Or you are highly sensitive, and your body has become a form of protection as 'armor' against energetic onslaught. Or there is some fear about what would happen if you achieved your goal weight.

There is always a positive pay-off to both your dream AND the fear associated with having it. On a piece of paper, draw a line down the middle from top to bottom and another from left to right—you will have four boxes. Label the rows as Get It and Fear, then label the columns with your Dream/Goal and then the Same or its opposite (what happens if you don't have or get it). See this example:

	Dream	Stay Same / Opposite of Dream
Get It		
Fear		

Now work through each box with the idea of understanding the positive pay-off of each square. What is the positive pay-off of getting your dream? Of staying the same or getting the opposite of your dream? For example, someone may dream of being slim *and* feel that people might judge them unless they stay the same.

Repeat the process for fearing your dream—what is the pay-off for being afraid about your dream? What is the positive pay-off for allowing fear to keep you in the same place or getting the opposite result?

There is always a positive pay-off to what we do and what we do not do in life. When you can reveal to yourself the positive pay-off that you may not know you are getting, you give yourself new choices and freedom to take different actions. And that's the Bigger Message...

Good Questions Yield Good Messages

When you actively seek out the Bigger Messages in your life, it can help to ask yourself questions—almost like an interview with yourself. The better the questions, the more valuable your answers. This happens when you talk with other people as well, right?

"How are you?" → "Fine."

"How are you doing since you got married and promoted within the same month?" → "Well, it's been a rollercoaster trying to catch up with myself and learn about..."

See the obvious difference? When you provide greater context to your questions, the answer can be much richer and more satisfying. When you ask yourself a question, make sure it is open-ended vs. a yes/no question, that it focuses on getting information you can use in your present life, and that it is objective so you don't beat yourself up for what you might now perceive as previous mistakes.

Right now, take a moment to reflect on the Bigger Messages present in your life. This requires just a few minutes of your time—it may be helpful to journal or doodle or diagram what comes up in your self-dialogue.

- What is the Bigger Message in this current situation? How does it look in a pattern?
- Is there a thread you want to unravel? Is there a pattern you want to change?
- What is your frame of reference for this situation? Is it valid for this situation?
- How can you view your current situation differently?
- As you look around your life, what are your current results?

- What results did you get that you wanted?
- What results occurred that you didn't want?
- What results haven't you noticed before?
- How can you make changes to live a bigger life?
- What is the significance of your instigating event right now?
- How large is the Bigger Message you're being invited to understand through your current experience?
- What can you do to see through the 'noise' more clearly to claim your clarity through your Bigger Message?
- What systems are needed to help you understand and live your Bigger Message once you understand them?

If you find after asking a question that you are getting a mushy, mixed, or partial Bigger Message, continue to go deeper with your questioning. One way to do that is to keep asking "what's under that?" and "what's under that?" You can also try mapping your answers by putting the question keyword in the center of a paper, then noting each answer around that keyword—it will look like a wheel with spokes coming from the center keyword. As you probe into each answer, write the keywords of those next-level answers around the original answer, again creating mini-wheels of association. Looking for the connections and insights using your senses, including visual and kinesthetic, can surface insights quickly because more of you is involved in the process.

The main idea is that the quality of answers you get from your reflection depends largely on the quality of the question asked as well as your intention in surfacing Bigger Messages. If your question is something like, "why would s/he do that?" or "who is to blame for my situation?", you are not asking quality questions because the answers are outside your control. Your questions must be about yourself, your experience, your options, your perception vs. those of any other person. You could ask "why would I do that?" or "how did I cause this situation?"—these are quality questions that will give you the clarity you seek.

That said, be open to the information that surfaces because you may not want to look at it, judge it as unattractive or undesirable in some way, or want it to be a different answer. In all cases, you are now responsible for what you have learned. It's not so much about the Bigger Message itself but what you decide to do about your discovery. You are always at choice...you can decide to do nothing, do something, or take on a major shift in some way.

You might want to seek counsel with a trusted friend, mentor, or family member; however, in that case, make sure to consider their point of view. Friends and family have one job—to love and, likely, protect you. Generally, they have their own distortions, judgments, projections, biases, and opinions because they are human. That doesn't mean they are wrong in anything they share with you; rather, they are sharing from their truth vs. what may or may not work for you. Whatever you decide must be based on your personal truth because you are the only one who will live with what you decide in the end.

The Keys to Manifesting What You Really Want

Manifestation literally is the result, or expression, of your power in alignment with your desires. What you manifest in life is an echo, or reflection, of the energy that you are putting out.

To power up your ability to manifest your intentional outcomes on the physical plane, there are principles you need to know *and* steps you can take to manifest deliberately.

The invitation within the act of intentional manifesting is that you attune yourself to match what it is that you want to attract. That is, if you want a good relationship, you must be good partner material.

There is always a matching picture to your vibrational frequency—it is that which manifests on the physical plane. It is what we call manifestation, but the reality is that the manifestation already exists—we are merely bringing ourselves to match it in order to experience it.

The Universe always seeks balance; the same is true whether it's the ebb and flow of the ocean or within an individual's life. Your life will be the sum total balance of the energy that you put out over your lifetime.

First, a definition...

Main Entry: man·i·fes·ta·tion

Pronunciation: "ma-n&-f&-'stA-sh&n, -"fe-'stA-

Function: noun

1 a : the act, process, or an instance of manifesting
b (1) : something that becomes tangible or exists in actualized form (2) : a perceptible, outward, or visible expression c : one of the forms in which an individual is manifested d : an occult phenomenon; specifically : MATERIALIZATION

2 : a public demonstration of power and purpose

Manifestation literally is the result, or expression, of your power in alignment with your desires. What you manifest in life is an echo, or reflection, of the energy that you are putting out.

To power up your ability to manifest your intentional outcomes on the physical plane, there are principles you need to know *and* steps you can take to manifest deliberately.

The invitation within the act of intentional manifesting is that you attune yourself to match what it is that you want to attract. There is an act of trust that is involved in the act of conscious manifestation, in that you know that the Universe has your back. When you trust yourself to create, you are trusting the Universe because the Universe is living through you. You are an expression of the Universe in physical form.

Additionally, as a result, you embody the power of all creation within you to create with intentional focus. There is no separation, or middleman, between where you are and what you want in your life. That said, there is a consciousness and a personal accountability required—and therein lies the rub. People often want change, but they don't want to do the work to have it.

MANIFESTING WHAT YOU REALLY WANT

You must know that you are worthy of receiving that which you want to manifest. There's a knowing within that is needed ... you must know that you can attract the outcomes you want *and* that you get to have them when they arrive. It's important to greet them with gratitude and accommodate your life around finally having them (for as long as you do). Being able to actually receive the expression of yourself in tangible form is not as easy as you think ... consider the last time you were really upset and needed a hug—and then got it. It's likely you cried even harder. ;+)

It's imperative that you recognize that whatever is manifesting in your life is a result of who you have been and where your energy was focused up until now. Receive it all with appreciation because it's clearly what was needed at some point; now that you have it, by embracing it, you empower yourself to create the new forms of your desires going forward.

In other words, if you cannot receive and embrace what you already have in your life, you dilute your power to manifest what you want going forward. It would be similar to acknowledging a new friend and then rejecting them because they are wearing a green shirt. How likely is it that you would attract a new friend if that is your reaction?

Energy is very literal—it takes the path of least resistance. If you don't want the new friend because they represent what you wanted then vs. now, the energy will move that person on into their next relationship without you. And then bring you someone who is the energetic match of your intention and presence. In that case, it may be someone who dresses appropriately but is judgmental and critical.

By the way, you cannot hate your way into manifesting what you would love to experience or have on the physical plane. If your energy is harsh, critical, or heavy, that will be the filter of what you will attract as everything must pass through and reflect those qualities to be in balance with you. In fact, even the things that people would label as 'bad' are here for your benefit. They show you the level of your personal energy frequency by bringing you the match of it. It's like a big mirror that when you understand how to use it for true sight, you can change the reflection to be what you want—that's what we think of as manifestation.

There are two more invitations for your personal self-mastery within the cycle of intentional manifestation.

One is to have compassionate detachment about the outcomes you experience. That is, you cannot be 'hooked' to having them show up in a particular time or form; rather, your role is to trust that whatever comes in is the highest form available to match your frequency. You must release your expectation and trust with an authentic knowing that your request will be fulfilled in the right time and form by the Universe.

The other is that you must become aware of your higher self, your connection to all that is, and the embodiment you are of universal intention. It's no mistake that you are here. You are a particle of a much greater consciousness. And when you know and honor that, you will discover a new life flow. By aligning with your highest possible vibration in every moment, your life will change (probably) dramatically. What you manifest will be supercharged in both timing and form. And you will experience less (if any) friction with the world around you.

Now you know the principles (or unchanging, timeless guidelines) of manifesting what you really want:

- Life is an echo of the energy you are putting out; you will manifest your match.
- You are the Universe living in physical form.
- Trusting yourself is trusting the Universe.

- The only separation between now and what you want is your personal vibration.
- You are continuously manifesting everything in your life.
- Gratitude is the highest frequency for (on-going) manifestation.
- You must know that you are worthy of your manifestations.
- Energy always takes the path of least resistance.
- Detachment allows you to receive the highest form of your desire.
- Manifestation is more powerful when you are in communion with your higher self.

In terms of how your focus on intentional manifestation will work throughout your life, read on...

Personal

When you are focused on being congruent with your higher self, making decisions from that vantage point, your life will take on a new level of ease. Your stress will be reduced, and you will be more comfortable within yourself.

At the same time, making a commitment to upgrade your manifestation results means not only handling what is in your world now but also cleaning up your energy field (or frequency). Your ability to create what you want will increase in proportion to the health and positivity of your habits, beliefs, perceptions, presence, self-responsibility, choices, and actions. At first, simply becoming aware of your habits will be enough to keep you in discovery; from there, you will find you can expand into new areas.

Once you take the path of the Bigger Message as it is presenting in your life, you cannot stay uninformed and negligent. You will begin to see your life through metaphysical eyes and take responsibility for who you are and what you are creating. It may not always be easy, but it is ALWAYS rewarding.

Environment

As you intentionally manifest, the 'container' of your life—your environment—will reflect your new outcomes. For example, you cannot manifest a six-figure job and continue living in a marginally decorated studio wearing hand-me-down clothing. What is around you is the barometer of your manifestation; therefore, your environment is critical to what you are creating.

You may begin your manifestation process by working with your environment. Decluttering, repairing, replacing items, and bringing in new décor that represents who you are now is the fastest path to creating new outcomes. Your inner belief systems cannot tolerate an imbalance between a beautiful outer environment and a shabby inner one, so your thoughts and beliefs will naturally shift to accommodate. The reverse is true as well…as you upgrade your self-talk and beliefs, your environment will upgrade in both appearance and functionality.

Career

Manifestation is a process of alignment. As a result, when you become more self-accountable to what you really want, and shift your mindset, behaviors, and support systems accordingly, your career will naturally expand to bring you to the right work.

If you begin your manifestation process with upgrading your career, it will affect the rest of your life. As you get into your right work (either by the employer, industry, or position), the compensation you receive will match your contribution. You will find that you are happier, make more money, and/or have better benefits, with people who you really enjoy. Remember, these circumstances manifest as a result of your willingness to transmute your energetic vibrational field into a match for them.

Health

Your physical health is a measure of your emotional, spiritual, mental, sexual, and energetic balance. Anything that is not resolved in any of those areas will present as an issue in your physical health. The good news is that once you have the symptom of any illness or disease, you can track back to your energy level that manifested it.

For example, a sore throat could mean that you haven't been speaking your truth. Cancer is a sign of suppressed anger, while epilepsy is a push-back to feeling fearful and overwhelmed. These are obviously sweeping statements! However, there is always a metaphysical insight to be discovered as a Bigger Message to any corresponding physical symptom.

When you become aware of the power of intentional manifesting, you also become aware of how your body has manifested by default what you were not aware of as it was happening. Where you did not have (or avoided) consciousness in manifesting, your body took the proverbial 'hit.' The good news is that you can intentionally manifest better health and greater vitality by handling the energetic frequency that caused the issue.

Relationships

When you intentionally manifest with awareness, you become happier. When you are happier, you are magnetically attractive to other people. Think of how you may have been single at one time, looking for a partner until you started dating someone—*then* all the wonderful options decided to come out of the woodwork! It's because you amped up your attraction frequency, which got traction with your partner—and became a signal for others who matched it to approach you.

Intentional manifesting can also have an effect on your existing relationships. Your loved ones, family, and friends may be thrilled with your outcomes... or they may be threatened. As you upgrade your life circumstances, it can be a trigger for their unseen or unresolved 'gunk.' They may feel left behind, or not good enough, or like they have to do something different or more in order to match your new levels of success. Their experience is theirs to have and your experience is yours to have... the invitation is to have authentic dialogue about what you each want to manifest (individually and together) going forward.

Recently, a client was upset that their friend had seemingly abandoned their relationship. Even more, he felt it wasn't the first time this had happened to him, and wondered if he was just that unlikeable. However, the reality is that it wasn't about his likeability; instead, it's about how congruent he was with that person—and congruence starts within. This is a Bigger Message that it was time to dig deep and consider with whom he was in relationships.

Something that many people don't realize is that the way they learned as children is often what they bring to their adult relationships. So, if you learned through pain and punishment, you would use that 'frequency' to transmit information to others. In a significant relationship, that can be damaging but you don't know it because it's so familiar to you. That's just one example of how unconscious, default programming can affect your current relationships.

Ask yourself:

- Who am I when I'm showing up in relationships?
- Do I express integrity in my communications and actions?
- What am I expecting from others? And am I willing to give it?

Typically, there are signs, or cues, from others in relationships that will tell us when to pay attention to something. Look to see if you're listening to what others are saying or assuming you understand, if you're re-treading the same types of issues in relationships, and/or where you tend to override what you know about the other person.

We teach others how to treat us and that includes your 'other.' They have likely given signals that were in a blind spot for you or were so unfamiliar that you didn't recognize them for what they were at the time.

By taking the time to evaluate your historical relationships and then to assess your current energetic state to make sure you're in integrity with your values, your health and your life purpose, you can determine if you're teaching others what you really meant for them to know about you. And you can further decide if you've been misinterpreting their signals in some way.

Relationships serve as our mirrors and can be one of the most powerful ways to grow ourselves. The Bigger Message is that you are accountable for what's happening in your relationships as they are a reflection of yourself.

Creativity

Creativity is not limited to artistic pursuits. When you realize that you can have whatever you truly desire, your creativity naturally rises to meet your potential. By inviting intentional manifestation into your life on a regular basis, you avail yourself to fresh sources of creativity, problem-solving, and life invention. Inspired insights spark your projects and infuse your thinking with new possibility. And seeing what used to be a 'challenge' becomes a new way to better yourself by creating breakthroughs.

Life Purpose

By focusing your ability to manifest on living your life purpose, you invite the Universe to express more fully through you, your gifts and natural talents, your desires and dreams.

Your life purpose is *not* found outside of you, in a job, as something that someone else told you is your life purpose. Your life purpose *is* the thing that lights you up, melts time and feels so right that you can lose yourself in it. It's not about money, or what other people say, or what comes of it... it's more important that you are expressing it daily.

For example, if you are blessed with a life purpose around teaching, you will find that you are the one who counsels your friends, explains what happened in a heated situation, helps the stranger find their way through your city with full directions, and writes out the recipe with specific details. You will naturally describe with clarity what is happening or what needs to be known in order to expand the knowledge base of your audience (or conversation partner). In other words, you will teach regardless of who, the subject, the circumstances, or payment... because it is your purpose.

Your life purpose is always expressing itself in one form or another. Intentional manifesting will reveal or illuminate it with greater precision because you will be lining up the circumstances to allow and support it more fully. As you are more satisfied with your life, there is a greater potential of flow for your life purpose. And your life purpose becomes more fully expressed the more that you align with your authentic desires.

Spend the next 27 days getting clarity, setting intention, shifting your mindset, and taking actions that will express your life purpose daily. As you do, become aware of the opportunities, relationships, and circumstances that you attract because they will be in greater alignment with your truth than ever before. Why 27 days? It's a number that comes from the practice of Feng Shui, symbolizing the energy of connection with collective consciousness, or higher power, in partnership to experience completion and fulfillment.

With the focus on manifesting, you can become more of who you are here to be on every level. Consider now this to be your invitation.

Why Are Some Things Easier to Manifest Than Others?

There are many reasons why this can be the case . . . for example, if your energy is not aligned with something you want to manifest, it cannot manifest for you until you are in alignment. The greater the gap, the more time required for manifestation.

If you are in touch with your consciousness, you likely know that energy can manifest on a quantum level; however, you are living on the physical plane which is dense and requires more time for manifestation. Rather than zipping from here to there, manifestation on the physical plane requires walking or running from here to there. When we align our energy with what we want, we are easily compelled toward it with the least amount of effort. And yet it still takes longer than on the etheric plane, which some part of your cellular structure may recall and, therefore, it seems more difficult on the physical plane.

When you are not attached to a particular thing manifesting, it is easier to manifest because you are not attached to the outcome. It is when you expect a certain thing in a certain way at a certain time with certain people that it takes longer—there are a lot of variables to line up. And if any of them change during the lining-up phase, everything changes so the process may have to start all over again.

When your intended desire is significant, there may be a lot of things that are needed to actualize it. For example, when you are looking for true love and are not interested in anything less, then it may take years to make that come to pass. Think of it like dinner... what takes longer—a Big Mac meal or a filet mignon prepared exactly to your taste?

If you change your intentions around your goals, it's like changing the way you've ordered a meal in a restaurant. For example, every time your order is underway for preparation, if there is a change in your request, everything has to shift to accommodate. Your clarity is a big key to conscious manifesting in a streamlined, efficient way.

If you're not thinking big enough, the Universe may have a hard time reducing your request into the thing you want. For example, if you're asking to get $10,000 but your destiny is $1,000,000, the Universe must shave down that bigger deliverable to match the size of your request. As another example, if you want to manifest a new home and you're thinking of a cute cottage, the mansion that was on the way needs to be pared down to match your request—and that will take longer.

Time is non-existent when it comes to manifesting—it is only our human perception of time that makes the process of manifestation seem longer or shorter. That said, focus on your clarity, visualization, intentions, release of what is in the way, and taking new actions to help make the process of conscious manifestation as efficient as possible.

It's important to clear space for manifesting what you truly desire. Release what no longer serves or supports you. Write a list of what you no longer need to carry with you in terms of beliefs, self-talk, judgments, perceptions... once it's written, light a candle and read them out loud with the intention of releasing them. Once you read them all, burn your list in the candle, then blow the candle out. Take extra time with your personal self-care to nurture yourself deeply. It is especially powerful to do this during a New Moon, which symbolizes new beginnings and is ideal for initiating intentional manifestation.

Here is another approach...like an archer who takes aim at a target, write your list of intentions for what you intend to manifest this month. Feel the power of what you intend to manifest build within you. Know with certainty that what you have visualized will come to pass. Allow your intentions to guide your thoughts, choices, and actions. Conscious manifesting requires both the framework and the follow through of your focus, mindset, and clarity. In the coming week, you'll want to act based on your stated intentions. Without intentions, you cannot take action. Without taking new action, you cannot manifest new results.

As another technique, visualize what you intend to manifest as though you already have it. How has your world changed? In what ways can you see that your intended result has manifested? What do you feel? By taking the time to visualize in your mind's eye your desired outcome, you are 'tuning' your energy state to match it energetically. You are strengthening the signal and showing your mind that it is already here; this is the pivot point as your mind will work to solve the gap of what is...it cannot have incongruence. You cannot have it so solidly fixed in your mind that it is not real on the physical plane.

This one action alone can supercharge your manifestation abilities, so take 11 minutes a day to visualize your successful manifestation as though it has already happened. Why 11 minutes? Eleven is the number of individual contributions (one plus one) to partnership (two) and making choices; in my world, this means partnership with a higher power, showing up on the physical plane and doing what I can do, and seeking options to make better choices. And if your visualization lasts longer than eleven minutes, great! You're giving that much more juice to your vision.

Altogether, you need to claim your desired manifestation with clarity and specificity. Remember that you do not get to state the 'how' it happens; therefore, it's best to limit your request to the outcome and accompanying details rather than the how and when of it. Today is a powerhouse day to release all the memories and distorted thinking about what it is that you want to experience. If you have anything in the way of thoroughly enjoying your desired outcomes, that is a great place to begin in terms of the release process. Take a moment to acknowledge that you are clear of what has held back your manifestations up until now. Be prepared to make new choices and decisions based on what you want vs. what's been historically.

To act in the physical world, find a treasure box that you can use to collect your visions, dreams, and desires. Note what you want to experience on individual pieces of paper, then place them in your treasure box. Place the treasure box under your bed at about heart level; that is, where your heart is when you are sleeping. This activates the energy to draw in what is needed to manifest your dreams. Know that this can surface new opportunities that you could have never predicted; be ready to take advantage of the ones that resonate with you.

Integrity Is Glue for Good Living

Just as a ship's hull requires integrity to be waterproof and strong against the powerful and ever-changing force of water, you need to have integrity in your life to be able to navigate the rigors of living it. Following are some of the qualities and characteristics of integrity:

- The state of being whole and undivided

- Firm adherence to a code of especially moral or artistic values (aka, incorruptible)
- An unimpaired condition (aka, being of 'sound' mind, body or state)
- The quality or state of being complete
- Expressing clearly aligned focus between thoughts and words, words and actions, beliefs, and behaviors.

When you have integrity, you are congruent in thought, word, and behavior. And it's what makes or breaks your success in life, even if that is all happening unconsciously.

You've experienced the opposite of integrity (or lack of integrity) with people who have broken promises to you, or situations that turned out different from their marketing and promotions, or vendors who didn't deliver as they said they would when you purchased from them.

A lack of integrity damages your credibility (with yourself and others), sets the stage for distrust going forward and feels repellant. When your life has a lack of integrity, multiply the negative consequences by a factor of 10—because it will create 10 times the negativity for you when you create, allow, or accept a lack of integrity in your life.

If someone makes an honest mistake, that's a different issue. That can be handled with communication, an apology, a new plan. However, if there is a true lack of integrity based on attitude, previous history, or greater circumstances, it is a different scenario entirely.

> *"The difficulty we have in accepting responsibility for our behavior lies in the desire to avoid the pain of the consequences of that behavior."*
>
> ~ M. Scott Peck

We are now in the Age of Aquarius, which is the astrological sign that connotes knowledge, revolution, and synthesis (or coming together) of systems. The stage for breakthroughs and self-realization is now set. Period.

Naturally, this applies to the integrity of your life. This means that whatever you are tolerating (putting up with) can be no more, whether that's relationships, lifestyle, occupation, or environment. Whatever changes need to be made for your optimal health and wellness are in motion whether you're ready or not—and this can manifest in unexpected ways. Anything that is out of alignment with integrity in your life will be revealed to be consciously addressed. Congruence between the inner and outer *will* be achieved.

What you focus your attention on is critical to what you are creating in your life and work like never before—you will manifest the deepest point of your focus. Clarity of perception is undeniable. You will be able to see dynamics, distortions, and discoveries without effort.

In other words, the Age of Aquarius is a revolution in consciousness. You, and only you, are completely responsible for your life experience. And it requires you to show up in integrity in every way. To help acclimate to this new level of consciousness, here are three things you can do.

ONE: Be accountable to yourself.

Determine where you have put off, delayed, stalled, or even allowed yourself to get stuck on achieving your goals or stepping into your next best level in life. Now, fair warning—once you honestly answer the questions below, you will need to act on what you discover. That action does not mean you need to do whatever it is that you said—yet. It means reconsidering if you still *want* to do that thing and, if yes, taking action in some way, including scheduling it, inviting others to help you, and working toward it in small increments, like five minutes a day.

- What projects have you put off?
- What projects need to be completed?
- What loose ends are plaguing you?
- What relationships require greater attention and integrity from you?
- What is unsaid for which you are the messenger?
- What are you tolerating in your life and work?
- What needs are you not meeting for yourself?

Now is the time for radical self-honesty. While it will shake up your world, it will make the shift easier because you're confronting it rather than reacting to it.

TWO: Express your dreams.

If there is something you want to know, do, be or experience, now is the time to express it. If your life, including health, relationships, work, isn't what you want it to be, what do you need to do differently?

This isn't about anyone but you—identify and articulate your dreams to start taking action on living them.

THREE: Understand what you are here to do.

You are unique in the fabric of time and space; you are here to contribute something valuable. Chances are that having your own business allows you the space and freedom to do it (but that's just me). ;+)

The truth is that your unique purpose is probably already expressing itself somewhere in your world even if you aren't an entrepreneur(yet). In any case, get clarity on what you are here to do and teach in the biggest sense to do it consciously.

Fair warning: if you do not step into your life with total integrity and make your distinct contribution, whatever that is, there will be a tsunami wave that will sweep through your life to release what you haven't yet addressed. And that's a lot more traumatic than doing it on your own proactively.

If you feel like every time you turn around there's something else that requires a new level of attention, that's because there is—life is speeding up. It may feel like you're being squished in the Tectonic plates of your life. In the moment, that can be a bit overwhelming but, in the end, doing the work now to align all the aspects of your life with integrity will make things flow easier and with greater intentional result for you in the long run.

Since we considered what intentional manifestation can look like in different areas of your life, let's consider what integrity looks like in various life areas to give you a sense of how following through on Bigger Messages with integrity can change your life.

Physical Body

Many people assume they know how to take care of their body because they've been living in it a long time. However, most of what we were taught even a generation ago is no longer considered 'best practices' for healthy, vital living. Not only have nutritional standards been upgraded, but so have the paradigms around exercise, rest, and meditation. Beyond that, each body is now considered unique in terms of what it needs—from minerals to hormones, blood type to metabolism, your body is its own ecosystem. And it's up to you to figure out what makes it run best.

The human body is designed to live for something like 200+ years but our life choices wear it out early. With proper care and feeding, you can live happier physically for a longer time now.

So, what does integrity with your body look like? Having consistent routines for everything from brushing and flossing your teeth to visiting the dentist, from eating every three hours to resting when you're tired, and sleeping for at least six hours a night gives your body the structural, nutritional, and active habits that keep you lean and your energy clean.

Be honest and consider where you are out of integrity with your relationship with your body. Then don't beat yourself up! Simply commit to new behaviors that honor your body as the vehicle that gets you through life every day.

Personal

The Bigger Message of being in tune with integrity in your life can change everything. Once you recognize that nothing is too small to be consciously aligned with the best version of yourself, you cannot just toss off a glib comment or procrastinate on a commitment.

The reality is that if you are lacking integrity in one part of your life, it's also showing up in at least one other area of your life. That means if you are late to meet a friend for drinks, you're likely late for other appointments too—and maybe even work. If you are breaking promises to others, you're breaking promises to yourself. And that does not set you up for success on any level.

When you decide to pay attention to how you're showing up in your life, you give yourself the gift of strength. Integrity is what strengthens all the aspects of your life, bringing them together as mirror aspects of their source—you.

The other aspect of integrity we need to address here is honesty. That is, do you speak your truth? Are you scrupulous about your standards of conduct so that people can rely on you, and they know it? Do you keep your word when you give it?

Having the courage to be honest with yourself and others gives you a greater capacity to have profound connections with others. People know when you're holding out, have expectations, are projecting your stuff and aren't showing up in your full potential and, naturally, in such cases, it's hard to trust you. However, when you are honest and demonstrate integrity in every area of your life, you naturally attract people's trust as the foundation for cultivating great relationships.

Environment

Your environment reflects your inner world. That is, what's 'out there' is 'in here' and vice-versa. So, if you look around at your environment and it doesn't match who you think you are, it's time to shake things up a bit.

The environment around you should be clean, functional, attractive, and comfortable for you. It should be a mirror of your interests, hobbies, personality, and lifestyle. If it isn't, either you've outgrown your environment or one of you needs an upgrade. ;+)

When it comes to evaluating the integrity of your space, begin with the biggest concept and work your way down to the specific as follows.

- Are you living in the right geographical area?
- Are you living in the right type of house or structure?
- Is the exterior of your home attractive and welcoming for you?
- Is the interior layout of your home conducive to the flow of your life?
- Is the décor attractive? Does the style suit you?
- Within each room, do you like the feeling and functionality of the furnishings in the room?

- Is there anything you would change about your furnishings, furniture, or artwork?
- Do you have clutter in any room? And, if yes, can you take care of it in less than an hour? (If yes, get it scheduled on your calendar and get it done!)
- Is there anything that needs to be repaired or replaced? If yes, make that a priority.

When you are in integrity with your environment, and your environment is integrity with supporting your best life, you will notice that shifts happen. The reason for that is because your environment is your outer body—as you take care of it, it will take care of you.

Your life needs a physical container to allow you to restore yourself so you can go out and make your contribution in the world. Make sure it's the best container you can create right now—then watch for synchronicities that show you that your desires are being manifested.

Career

When you choose to invest your productivity must be congruent with what you care about as well as your unique talents and strengths. Why? Because if you are doing something you don't care about or that you aren't strong in, you are doing it only for the money—and that's not enough to truly motivate you to show up fully. It's also not the way to know that you're making a meaningful difference in the world.

Your work needs to be in integrity with who you are, what you're good at, and where you want to make a bigger difference. When you commit to being in integrity through your work, your position and/or job will take on a fresh flavor for greater performance and personal fulfillment.

If you are not contributing to something greater than you while using your natural talents, you are stunting yourself. If you are not in the right career, handling the right kinds of responsibilities for the right employer, it will cause you stress and, more than likely, problems at work.

If you are in the right place doing the right things with the right employer situation, the next question becomes are you showing up fully in integrity with what you know you can do? If you are holding back, find yourself complaining or looking for a new job or career option, you are out of integrity in your career.

When you get into integrity with your career, you are naturally motivated to add to your skills set, go further on a project, and like to take on new responsibilities because you know that you are making a significant difference. Let now be the time that you assess the degree of integrity between your professional life and your personal desires and talents and, if there is a gap, acknowledge it and start closing it.

Health

> *"When health is absent, wisdom cannot reveal itself, art cannot manifest, strength cannot fight, wealth becomes useless, and intelligence cannot be applied."*
>
> ~ Herophilus

When you are incongruent, or out of integrity, in any part of your life, your body will experience dis-ease (either in terms of stress or through illness). It is a foundational energy loss because, as you sense you are making choices that don't support your best and highest self, it becomes an energetic drag. In turn, that creates an unnecessary waste of mental energy.

If you think of a large backpack full of the things you are lacking integrity with sitting heavily on your back throughout your day, you can imagine the relief of removing that backpack and the energy that would return for other things in your life. When you have integrity with your personal goals and choices, you create the conditions for optimal life force energy through your health.

Being out of integrity leads to stress and stress is the #1 cause of most illnesses today. You know what you need to do to take care of your health. If you're not doing it, it's time to get honest and consider the greater pay-off you're having from not taking care of yourself. Clearly there is something that is preventing you from honoring yourself, which causes fundamental stress, which takes a toll on your health. Once you identify that root cause for your behavior, you give yourself new options for better health.

In case you are experiencing a lack of optimal health right now, there is a Bigger Message for you in that experience. It's inviting you to look beyond the symptoms to see what's really going on and make some changes in your life. Your health is the barometer of how you're handling stress, how effectively you're restoring your energy, and the sum total of all the little energy drains that can happen over the course of daily living. Pay attention to get into integrity so you can enjoy more vital health every day.

When you're feeling strong and healthy, it's easier to follow through on everything in your life. When you are in integrity in your own self-care, you are unstoppable. Take the time to assess how you feel in your body. If there is anything that is unbalanced (and you will know what that is), make plans to address it this week. If your body wants better nutrition or to move more, you can do that right away. Your integrity to yourself is the key to living a good life—why throw that away with bad habits, unaddressed issues, neglect or just being lazy? Love yourself enough to be disciplined in how you care for yourself, and your life will pay you back for it.

Relationships

Your relationships are a match to the energy that you are putting out. When you are in integrity, congruent with your beliefs and values, speaking your truth, and showing up fully to participate in a relationship by taking ownership of your own emotional wellness, your relationships are more engaging and fulfilling.

However, when you are out of integrity in your relationships (including the one you have with yourself), you set the stage for misunderstandings, miscommunications, and missed opportunities. Ironically, this is the time when you can most grow from your relationships because these are your disguised invitations for growth.

Over time, your relationships will change; in fact, they must, to keep up with your evolution. If you find that you have 'unfinished business' with a relationship or past occurrence with another person, it keeps you out of integrity and that will affect other areas of your life.

It is vital you feel supported by your relationships, whether with family, a significant other, a best friend, social circle, colleagues, vendors . . . anyone in your world who has some relationship with you by your definition and allowance (as they are in YOUR world). You can see how you are showing up by observing who is entering your world and how your relationships are changing.

People who have poor boundaries often struggle in relationships. This is a symptom of poor integrity with self because boundaries are not honored by others—others have taught them how to treat themselves as a second-class citizen. That means, as an adult, they do not put themselves first. When that person learns their value and to get their needs met and say no to what doesn't serve them, relationships become much cleaner. When you honor your boundaries, so can others. When you don't know how to honor your boundaries, most people find it easier to sacrifice the relationship than grow themselves with integrity and 'own' their part in the relationship dynamic.

In short, consider your relationships and ask yourself how you feel about each one. Notice if you feel good more often than not after seeing that person, if you are participating fully in the relationship or if you are holding back in some way. Notice what fulfills you and what doesn't, then take action to see that your needs get met. That may occur through clear communication and making a request, or it may be through attracting a new relationship. Whatever the relationship, come from a place of integrity to allow each of you to show up in your full capacity—the key to the most rewarding kind of relationship regardless of the type.

Creativity

When your life is in integrity with your values, beliefs, thoughts, and behaviors, you have more energy. Your desire to create something new increases and, without the stress of managing incongruence, you feel lighter, so you have the energy to do it. With expansive space in your energy field, your creativity begins to express itself in new ways.

Creativity is not limited to the arts (painting, music, etc.). Creativity is in how you see the world, the way you approach solving problems, the perspective you have on your relationships as you see with fresh eyes. Life is more spontaneous, and you enjoy new freedom in every way—including your creativity.

Interestingly enough, the best creativity happens when you assign integrity to it. For example, if you wanted to create (write) a new book, the best way to make that happen is to give yourself deadlines. Why? Because if you don't, you'll never have a sense of urgency to actually do it!

So, creativity will benefit by having integrity in how you approach it and the parameters you use to create an actual outcome. And you may decide to not have an outcome—instead, you may decide that you're going to play for one afternoon and see what happens. That's what a major technology company does—they give their engineering team 24 hours every quarter to work on their own projects and see what happens. Giving employees creative freedom is why we now have Post It notes, I do believe. The glue for Post Its was originally a failed batch of glue meant for aerospace and the formula sat for about five years until someone started playing with it and, seven years after that, Post Its were born.

At any rate, being in integrity leads to greater creativity and giving your creativity a structure of some sort creates the space for something new to emerge. (Kinda makes you want to go create something now, doesn't it?) ;+)

Life Purpose

Webster's Definition of Congruence: "Congruence is the quality or state of agreeing or coinciding; state achieved by coming together, the state of agreement."

When you are living in integrity with whom you are here to be and the unique purpose you are to fulfill, your life has meaning and generates a deep sense of contentment within.

Every decision you make defines you and makes you who you are—including how on track you are with your individual life purpose.

Life purpose is not found in a job or from something someone else says you are to do. Instead, it is what pulls you forward naturally—the thing that may seem too easy because you are usually doing it in some form consistently throughout your life.

> *"It is not who I am underneath, but what I do that defines me."*
> ~ Batman

Being aligned with your life purpose is one of the ultimate hallmarks of success because it will give you energy, melt obstacles, and create opportunities without effort. Conversely, when you are not in integrity with your true-life purpose, your work feels like, well, work! You are not as interested as you could be, get side-tracked by challenges and distractions, and do not go the extra mile in how you show up for projects.

In this case, the best thing you can do is take some time to consider how you feel when you know you are aligned with something (usually that means happy, light, and optimistic). When you have that feeling in mind, think about your life and the times you've felt that feeling—especially when working. That will give you a new approach to find clues about how your life purpose has expressed itself in the past so you can find new ways to express it going forward.

Your integrity is the tie that binds you and what you experience in life. Essentially, integrity means strength and solidarity. When you are congruent and aligned with your values, beliefs, thoughts, words, and behavior, you have less (or even no) stress in your life because you are fully expressing yourself. Even more, people will be drawn to your clarity and presence. Look for the areas in your life that are experiencing stress and you will find your invitations to step into greater integrity.

Life is an echo—what you put out is what you get back. That is decidedly true in the relationships in your life. You can see who you were at different points in your life based on who you attracted into it then. When you live from your own integrity, you speak your truth, and show up without hesitation. You will also feel centered enough in yourself to ensure your emotional needs are met so that you do not project them on to other people. In other words, when you have integrity, you are responsible with your energy. As a result, you experience cleaner and more fulfilling relationships. Consider any conversations that you need to have and just get them done—it will get things back on track with the people in your life.

One other point... you cannot attract that which is not part of your energy field—that is the state of being in integrity. Whatever you are aligned with is what you experience. What you are is what you attract—it cannot be any other way. And that includes abundance in all forms—money, prosperity, good friends, opportunities, etc. So, if you want to make more money, increase your integrity around it. Make sure you have a budget, that you know your debts and have a plan for paying them off, pay your bills on time and be responsible with your money. If your money was your friend, are you honoring it right now? Get into integrity around your finances and watch them grow.

All in all, this is a good time to get into integrity with yourself on all levels of your existence. Know that when you do, you might make some people unhappy. That's because they know you as they do and your shift will force them to shift too in order to stay in relationship with you. If they are meant to be in your life going forward, that will happen with your mutual intention. (And if not, you will need to choose between releasing them or staying smaller than you were designed to be in this lifetime.)

Commit to What You've Learned

Most people betray themselves more than they do anyone else by saying one thing (even with best intentions) and then doing another. When someone else makes you a promise and then breaks it, you know the pain and it usually affects your relationship in some way. That same scenario is even bigger within you for yourself. It can cost you faith and trust in your decisions and undermine your self-esteem.

Whatever you neglect to respect is a self-betrayal. And that is about not having the internal support to accomplish what you said you wanted to do, especially if it's something new.

Begin changing the tide of honoring your self-commitments by forgiving yourself for what you haven't done in the past. Know that you did the best you could with whatever the circumstances and let yourself off the hook. After all, it's hard to push for a new commitment when the old self-blame blocks progress.

Then make small commitments that you honestly know you can do. These are promises that you know you can keep. Make one small commitment for your own self-care daily and honor that for this month; in 21 days, you will have a new habit. Then next month, make another small commitment for change and, once it's a habit, make another small commitment. Note: if you make too large a commitment too fast, your reptilian brain will stop or sabotage you as an ancient protection mechanism. It's not worth it—stay small and steady to create positive change.

But what happens when you can't keep a commitment? Or worse, you totally fail at it?

There is a difference between keeping a commitment and honoring a commitment. There are some commitments that you cannot keep, no matter how hard you try—but you can still honor them.

Keeping a promise means 'the letter of the law' of the promise, while honoring a promise means it's about the spirit of the promise. It's possible to honor a promise without keeping it, and you can keep a promise without honoring it (which is the greater travesty). To honor your commitments, you need three things: respect, communication, and productive effort.

Consider your outstanding commitments to yourself and then to others. Where are you lacking respect for that commitment? Where do you need additional communication about that commitment to honor or keep it? What action(s) do you need to take to be in integrity with that commitment?

Once you identify areas that need your attention, take the time to follow through on them this week—it will give you freedom in (possibly unexpected) new ways. Over-committing yourself doesn't help anyone—least of all yourself. You might find yourself frustrated, anxious, or stressed (especially at this time of year!). Maybe you didn't think things through before you promised something or you forgot about something you had already committed to or you shouldn't have made the commitment in the first place…in any case, the first response is usually to just try powering through it—and that doesn't usually give great results.

Sometimes there are genuine challenges to keeping a commitment—maybe a traffic jam, or someone else was supposed to do something before you could do something, or a vendor was out of the product you said you would get from the store. You can't do much about these situations; your only way through is to communicate as quickly as possible the situation to the other people involved so they have the same information as you and can re-set their expectations.

Consider potential over-commitments in your schedule right now. Chances are you can take at least 20% of the activities out of your calendar and nothing would change for the final outcomes—but it would give you breathing room. Where are you committed to things that shouldn't be on your schedule? Where are you not accounting for something—like drive time or another person's performance? Go through your schedule and delegate or eliminate what isn't serving you. Then schedule the commitments you need to follow through on as well as any conversations you need to have with others.

It may be uncomfortable to admit that you've been over-committed but it's easier than facing disrespect or disappointment. Even if you haven't honored a commitment up until now, 'own' that through honest conversation to get back on track.

Then, be realistic, honest, and clear in setting your commitments (or asking them of others). It's better to realistically set expectations and realize you cannot do it than to trick yourself into something that you cannot follow through on effectively.

When establishing a commitment, be sure to consider more than the bare minimum as you don't want to undersell the task at hand. For example, if you want to start getting in shape, you may think, "I just need to go to the gym," *but* if that has not worked in the past, it may mean hiring a trainer, following a prescribed protocol, attending classes at certain times, writing out your results or more. A commitment means giving your all to see something through...so (especially at this time of year) be realistic about what you're committed to and about what you are actually willing to do to make it happen.

Give yourself the gift of clarity in your commitments. Where are you under-selling them? Where are you rationalizing about your ability to do them? Where do you need support to get them done? Or are there commitments that you simply need to release because they are no longer a priority?

Once you assess your commitments and release what isn't working, you give yourself more energy to follow through on the commitments you want to keep to yourself and others. That honors the sacred bond of commitment that supports you and—bonus!—everyone else in your world benefits too.

By having a finite time frame, like twelve months, you give yourself a container into which you can pour all your intentional efforts. By having clarity around what you really want, you can discern whether this is a worthy use of your time, energy, and resources. And then, by making a commitment, you choose to have what you desire beyond being merely interested in having it. A commitment means you will do what it takes to have what you truly want.

Use the next couple of days to review the outstanding commitments from this past year. Are there any that you need to bring forward into the new year or can you let them go? Whatever you need to bring forward, write on a piece of paper. Then consider what new commitments you would like to make for the coming year. Take the time to really look at what you want in your life to be different and what it will take to make that happen. Write down the commitments that you want to consider for the coming year.

Now go through your list with brutal honesty. Consider the outcome (is it worth it?), cost of getting (do you need to invest?), ease of implementation (what will it take from you to have this?) and, once that's done with each of your potential commitments, determine your top three commitments for the next year. You can hold on to the other ones in case you achieve your top three commitments sooner! But, for now, you will have your focus *only* on three commitments at the most.

A commitment is different than a resolution, by the way. You can blow off a resolution. But a commitment means consistent, unwavering, unrelenting focus for your time, mindset, energy, and resources. You are putting these commitments to creating something new ahead of anything else that may come up because you will do what it takes to have them regardless of circumstances.

Now What?

Now that you understand more about the language of your Bigger Messages as they speak to you through your life and have a sense of what the symptoms might mean, the big question becomes: what do you do to gain access to a higher level of awareness? If you don't change, you will get the same results you've gotten previously.

The good news is that your transformation has already begun because you have a new perspective based on what you've just read here. That said, there are other things you can do to entrain your boldest life into reality faster and easier.

1. Act on what you learn with detachment to the actual outcome.

Consider it as though you just got a new smartphone. Your task is to learn about your phone, what the buttons do, how the commands work, add your apps . . . and in that process, sort out whatever you encounter. You are flexing with situational needs vs. thinking only of how great your phone will be when it's fully programmed. In fact, if you think too far ahead, you might miss a prompt and get tangled up in commands . . . you might accidentally do a total reset on what you just programmed!

Even more, you might add apps because they catch your eye, the benefits are enticing, or all your friends have it (which are all primary reasons why many people do most things in life). Over time, you determine which ones you actually use, love, and benefit from and then delete the others . . . or at least you should delete the others because they take up space, energy (battery life), and attention. Again, these double as good reasons to get rid of things that no longer serve you in real life.

By focusing on staying present and doing what needs to be done, you create the outcome you want—your customized smartphone. Applying this Bigger Message to your life means taking action toward your best life and then being present to what you need to do and know as you go to create it.

2. Consider your social environment.

It's important that you are surrounded with people who can offer meaningful, positive support. If that's not occurring, it's like a fish trying to swim in sand. Hang out with people who 'get' you and want you to succeed in living your best, boldest life.

3. Stay calm and self-contained about what's happening in the moment to bring you your Bigger Message.

In other words, avoid 'leaking' emotionally. If you have drama, chaos, or feel the need to overshare someone else's information, you're leaking. We humans psychologically leak when we have too much to hold in our minds—it must come out somewhere and it will find a way when we least expect it. Find a safe way to get that handled vs. spontaneously leaking or being emotionally messy. Aim for personal equanimity, or balance, even in stressful situations.

4. Relax into the uncertainty when receiving or decoding a Bigger Message.

If you can tolerate the not-knowing as your 'jumping off' place to where you're going in living your boldest life, things flow, and you can handle pretty much anything. That's also a great starting place to practice confidence while demonstrating your resilience and your trust in your transformation process.

5. We live in a positive universe; that is, everything is intended to promote life and flow and negative energy detracts from creating and expanding life.

If you focus on the negatives through your thoughts, language, choices and behaviors, there is a cosmic assumption that you want more of what you're focusing on. For example, if you are focused on "I don't want to mess things up," you're basically setting the homing device to call 'messing things up' into your life! Watch your own messaging for what you're focused on and calling in to you. And think about your future with optimism—where you are now is not a predictor of where you will be. It's really basic cause and effect—so get positive to attract your best life!

6. Communicate clearly and with personal integrity.

Say what you mean, mean what you say, and ask for what you want. This will help develop and support more meaningful relationships as well as focus your intentions accurately. If you need details, ask for them—don't put the responsibility for your clarity on someone else. Recognize your role in creating relationships with people *and* with what you want through the language you choose and the connections you create through your communication skills.

7. If you're in a tough spot, reframe what is happening in a way that acknowledges the growth opportunity.

Understand that if you are challenged, it is a message that it's time for you to grow beyond where you've been. In fact, you could even look at this as a healing, since anything that's happening now reflects old patterns that need to be expressed and released. Ask yourself: "What is the greater opportunity here?" "What is the positive meaning behind what's going on?" "What strengths do I have to handle this situation well?" "How can I be grateful for what's happening now?"

Once you know the Bigger Message of the current situation and/or have some insight about what it all means, you can go beyond it to see how that could be showing up in other areas of your life—simply identifying the pattern and where it shows up releases some of the energy that isn't supporting you right now. Reframing distills the essence of what you need to get from it to move on more quickly.

Finally, remember that you are the one in charge of manifesting your results in life—what you get is what you expected to get, regardless of what you said you expected to get. Your perception matters, your attitude makes a difference, and the thought of origin underlying anything is the true compass steering you to the results you are focusing on. Clarity is your key to manifesting. It is your personal choice that dictates the outcomes of receiving, understanding, and acting on your Bigger Messages.

Living from your Bigger Message(s) means honoring the fact that you are invaluable and a very necessary part of something much greater. By seeing how you are affecting the world around you and consciously cultivating your awareness of your presence and then how you are engaging with the greater whole through every circumstance, situation, and relationship, you give yourself the gift of your best life.

You *are* the power to create your most amazing life! By following your Bigger Messages, you deliberately shift your inner state to more easily follow the roadmap that literally unfolds at your feet as you walk it to your greater destiny.

Here's to understanding the universal context—the Bigger Messages—of your life so you can live your best life now.

Bonus Gifts

Finding the true meaning of the events and circumstances in your life is what releases you from the past and allows you to move forward. Whatever the event, it occurs to give you more clarity to move you forward to the next opportunity. The good that comes out of the 'bad' things (which are usually just unexpected) that happen to you helps you become your best, most authentic self.

> *"Nothing is good or bad—'tis only our thinking that makes it so."*
>
> ~ William Shakespeare

There are ten significant reasons behind the things that happen—each is a different way of helping you become your best self. And YOUR reason is the specific message that you need to do a better job leading the life you were meant to lead as the person you were meant to be. Things happen to help you get rid of the parts of yourself that aren't you; to help you be more real and more yourself, not like everyone else; to help you lead a more authentic life, and, ultimately to help you discover who you really are.

Discover these reasons—the Bigger Messages—for yourself when you download your free ebook—*Everything Happens for a Reason*—today.

lynnscheurell.com/reasons-message

And, as promised, you'll find the Companion Guide there as well. :+)

About the Author

I'm Lynn Scheurell. When I was seventeen, I was in the throes of wanting to know what I was supposed to do with my life. I would ask that question to people, my higher power, my environment... it was a huge deal for me. I just *had* to know *why* my life would matter when I was living on purpose. That was when I heard 'the voice'—the epiphany that became my life's guiding star. The message was to 'actualize potential.' That might seem like a wide-ranging mission, but it helped me to focus my attention, gifts, skills, energy, and work toward facilitating positive transformation in the lives I touch, from colleagues to clients.

Personally, one of my goals became to never have regrets and have good memories in my golden years so I did everything that held any interest for me. I was a wrangler and rodeo barrel racer in Wyoming. I saw the statue of David in Rome, ate potato pizza in a terrazza, and threw coins in the Trevi Fountain. I held my breath in the sacred silence of Notre Dame, felt small next to the Nike statue, rode the TGV to visit chateaus, and had espresso with friends in a café on the

Seine River. I've visited all of Leonardo daVinci's homes. I pressed my nose on glass to be inches from King Tut's mask. I drove a vintage Jeep through the countryside of Guadalajara. I had afternoon snacks with breathtakingly beautiful views near Lake Guatavita, home of the Colombian Loch Ness. I partied with local reggae musicians in Ocho Rios. I took a ferry in Stockholm, touched the Jarlabanke Runestones in Täby, and witnessed the changing of the guard at the Swedish palace. I became a professional ballroom dancer and, upon finding myself partnerless, discovered the profound joy of belly dancing. I wanted to share the thrill of embracing all that life offers so I started writing; that led me to becoming a certified book coach and bestselling author.

Professionally, I had mainstream jobs as my primary income source. I did everything from restaurant management to physician recruiting to paying medical health claims to running a temp agency for insurance professionals. I worked in the nonprofit sector as a Director of Development and then was a Dean of Education in a for-profit system for a while. I've been a digital strategist and copywriter for Fortune 100 companies, visionary startups, and entrepreneurial ventures. My resume now has a 'thud' factor which, at one time, was definitely not cool. Interviewers either saw my experience as 'froggy' or as a 'thoroughbred'—now it serves me well because I can relate to so many different personalities, industries, and environments.

Speaking of which, at the same time I was trying to maintain a semblance of living between the corporate lines, I also had many side hustles. I had a retail boutique called Nouveau Ritz that was as fun as the name sounds... and a Feng Shui business that helped clients open to their true nature and live their dreams. Eventually, my business became about helping people identify their life purpose and translate it into viable business models, compelling messaging, and

ABOUT THE AUTHOR

valuable signature systems. Ultimately, that evolved into teaching entrepreneurs and business owners about the art of change and personal transformation for self-mastery through business.

From all this deep experience, I understand the complexity and rewards of discovering and living with authenticity. Where it can be easy to stay frozen in fear, I have learned how to embrace change through claiming personal power even when the world is in chaos. Life is not a direct path to success; instead, it is what we choose to experience that makes it successful. And now that is what I teach through my life's work.

The reality is that clarity is power, and truth opens new doors. By going beyond one's own myths, the possibilities become endless and exciting. Challenges are opportunities for growth. Business is the fast-track to accelerated personal growth. Change is natural and necessary evolution vs. a reason to fear. Bold choices reflect faith and a willingness to be open to what life can bring. And I'm there for my students and clients to see and help guide their unique experience with anticipation.

For now, I'm happy to be in your world in some way. May my books bring you insights, and life bring you only good things.

LynnScheurell.com

Other Books by Lynn Scheurell

You've Arrived!: A 5-Step System to Bypass Your Logical Mind, Activate Your Intuitive Potential and Gain Perfect Clarity For Your Business

The Energy of Money: How to Understand and Quantum Leap Your Relationship with Money Using Metaphysical Insights

Feng Shui for Entrepreneurs: Harnessing the Power of Your Environment for Business Success

Defining Your Purposeful Prosperity Path: How to Make Opportunities, a Business Model and a Living from Your Wisdom

www.ingramcontent.com/pod-product-compliance
Lightning Source LLC
Chambersburg PA
CBHW072059290426
44110CB00014B/1741